DATE DUE

Reprints of Economic Classics

RURAL ECONOMY IN NEW ENGLAND
AT THE BEGINNING OF THE 19TH CENTURY

RURAL ECONOMY

IN NEW ENGLAND

AT THE BEGINNING OF THE

I9TH CENTURY

BY

PERCY W. BIDWELL

[1916]

AUGUSTUS M. KELLEY • PUBLISHERS
CLIFTON 1972

First Edition 1916

(New Haven: Transactions of the Connecticut Academy of
Arts and Sciences, Volume XX, 1916)

Reprinted 1972 by
Augustus M. Kelley Publishers
REPRINTS OF ECONOMIC CLASSICS
Clifton New Jersey 07012

. . . .

I S B N 0-678-00815-9
L C N 68-55480

. . . .

PRINTED IN THE UNITED STATES OF AMERICA
by SENTRY PRESS, NEW YORK, N. Y. 10013

TRANSACTIONS OF THE

CONNECTICUT ACADEMY OF ARTS AND SCIENCES

VOLUME 20, PAGES 241-399   APRIL, 1916

Rural Economy in New England at the Beginning of the Nineteenth Century

BY

PERCY WELLS BIDWELL, PH.D.
Instructor in Economics in Yale University

NEW HAVEN, CONN.
1916

TABLE OF CONTENTS.

PREFACE.

The following chapters are a part, only, of a larger work which I have undertaken, a history of the changes in the rural economy of New England in the nineteenth century. In broad outline such a history falls into three periods: (1) The period of self-sufficient economy, which had existed since the settlement of the country, reaching the highest point of its development at the beginning of the nineteenth century; a period in which the characteristic features of rural economy were the absence of any market for farm produce and the consequent dependence of each town and, to a large extent, of each household, even, on its own resources for the satisfaction of its wants. (2) The period of transition to commercial agriculture, under the stimulus afforded by the rise of manufacturing enterprises in inland towns and villages and the consequent demand for food and raw materials on the part of the newly-arisen non-agricultural population; the years included in this period being approximately the two generations from 1810 down to the close of the Civil War. (3) The period of the decadence of New England agriculture, extending from the close of the Civil War to the end of the nineteenth century; a period in which the increasing pressure of Western competition caused the abandonment of large numbers of New England farms and a decline in both the quantity and quality of the rural population. It was thus that the Rural Problem of New England arose. From an appreciation of the importance of the problem have arisen organized efforts looking toward its solution, toward an economic and social rehabilitation of rural life in this region.

The chapters here presented constitute a survey of the rural economy of the three states of southern New England at the close of the first period.

I desire to make acknowledgment of the courtesies extended to me by the librarians of the American Antiquarian Society, the Connecticut Historical Society, and of the Harvard and Yale University libraries. My thanks are due also to various members of the Department of Economics of the Graduate School of Yale University, and also to Professor F. W. Taussig of Harvard University, for encouragement and helpful suggestions.

In a very especial manner I am indebted to the late Professor Guy S. Callender, of the Sheffield Scientific School of Yale University, who directed my researches in this field. Without his helpful advice, his illuminating criticism and his stimulating companionship this book could not have been written.

PERCY WELLS BIDWELL.

New Haven, January 1, 1916.

INTRODUCTION.

It is the purpose of this essay to analyze the economic conditions of life in inland towns in southern New England a century ago, with a view to showing in what way, and to what extent, these conditions were effective in shaping the peculiar features of home and community life of this region at the time. In other words, it is our aim in the first place to discover what were the most important circumstances which affected the ability of the inhabitants of these towns to produce wealth, that is, to satisfy their wants, to get a living; and in the second place, to show in what ways these people sought to adapt themselves to their circumstances so as to satisfy their wants most easily, to get the best living possible.

The townships into which the area of Massachusetts, Rhode Island and Connecticut was at this time divided were more than convenient geographical divisions for administrative purposes; they were units of economic and religious as well as of political life. Inside these economic microcosms, these cells of the social organism, there were developed distinctive individual habits and characteristics, and distinctive social customs. The stern austerities of New England character have often caused comment and discussion, as have also the remarkable energy, industry and ingenuity of its people. So also the peculiar unity and cohesion of their social and religious life are well-known and accepted facts. But the interest of most students and writers in these matters has been that of the mere antiquarian. A detached fact, an isolated idea, concerning the life of the early settlers of this region has been picked up and examined with enthusiastic interest and with a certain kind of appreciation, such as a connoisseur of antiques might display when rummaging for old crockery or furniture through the attic of a farmhouse. Rarely has there been an attempt at real economic history; that is, at an explanation, a synthetic reconstruction of the way in which these people got their living. To do this all these scattered, and of themselves interesting facts must be fitted together, must be brought into some orderly relation showing cause and effect; they must be interpreted in the light of the fundamental principles of economic theory. In this essay such an attempt at reconstruction and interpretation will be made.

As a field for a study in economic history no region offers better opportunities than do the three states of southern New England at the beginning of the nineteenth century. Here we find an "economic province," a territory of uniform life based upon a uniform physical environment, peopled by a homogeneous race, with common descent, common traditions, and common institutions. This uniformity of conditions gives the student the great advantage of being able to draw general conclusions for the whole region from the evidence presented in typical localities. He has, moveover, the advantage of investigating an approximately static condition in economic life. For at least a generation, there had been practically no change in the manner of life of the inhabitants in most of the towns. In many of the older towns there had been little change in 50 or 100 years. The process of pioneering was finished, practically all of the land which was then considered available had been brought under cultivation; in the current phrase, these states were "fully settled." But a great change was impending; soon the familiar, stereotyped ways of doing things, traditional habits of life and of thought were to suffer modification and in a few generations were to disappear almost entirely. The revolutionary force was to come from the rise of manufactures and the growth of a non-agricultural population in the inland towns. It is peculiarly interesting and instructive to examine the economic and social life of these communities at this critical stage in their history.

The general plan of the essay may be outlined as follows: In the first place an analysis of the occupations of the inhabitants of the inland townships will be undertaken. Not only will the relative importance of each trade, business, and profession be determined, but also the nature of the relations existing between each and the agricultural industry will be considered. In other words, this portion, Chapter I, will be devoted to a study of the extent of the Division of Labor in the inland townships.

The second step, Chapter II, will be to determine how far the inland communities thus described were typical of the whole region of southern New England. A search will be made for industrial and commercial towns and the commercial relations between these and the purely rural towns will be considered.

In Chapters III and IV an attempt will be made to find out how far these rural communities engaged in commerce with the inhabitants of regions outside New England. An investigation will be made of the extent of the demand for foodstuffs in the Southern states and in the West Indies. To determine how far this market was supplied by farmers in inland towns, an examination of the conditions of internal trade and of the transportation system in southern New England will be necessary.

Thus far we have been employed in describing the economic conditions, in reconstructing the environment in which the inland farmers found themselves. The second part of the essay, Chapters V and VI, will be devoted to describing the state of the agricultural industry as carried on by inland farmers, and the general features of life in the home and in the community. Finally, these facts will be brought into relation with those of the economic situation that we have described in the first four chapters.

CHAPTER I.

THE INLAND TOWNS AND THEIR VILLAGE SETTLEMENTS.

The typical inland township in southern New England in 1810 was an area of roughly 40 square miles,[1] containing a population of from 1,000 to 3,000 persons. An examination of the Census of 1810 shows us 385 of such towns, out of a total of 437. Of the remaining 52 towns only three[2] had as many as 10,000 people, 11 had between 5,000 and 10,000 and 38 varied from 3,000 to 5,000. More significant than these figures as showing the predominant importance of the smallest towns is the fact that 67 per cent, or more than two-thirds of the total population, lived in these; one-quarter in towns of from 3,000 to 10,000 people, and only about one-sixteenth of the total number in the largest towns.[3] Within the group of the smallest towns, considerable variations in size were to be found. In newly settled or in unfertile regions, such as Berkshire and Worcester counties in Massachusetts, a large proportion of the towns contained from 500 to 1,500 people. On the other hand, in especially fertile districts, as, for instance, in the Connecticut valley,[4] or where an old town had retained a large grant of land unsubdivided, as, for instance, Farmington and Saybrook,[5] the population ranged between 2,500 and 3,000 or above. On the whole, however, we shall find that all the towns in this group which we have selected as the typical inland towns show characteristics which set

[1] The variations from this norm were considerable, especially in the longer settled regions where the older towns had been often subdivided. Some of the towns, also, had acquired and kept unusually large grants of land. Consequently, towns as small as 20 square miles or as large as 70 are sometimes found. The best source of information as to the area of towns at this time is Pease and Niles, Gazetteer of the States of Connecticut and Rhode Island. Hartford. 1819. We have no similar work at this date for Massachusetts, except for individual towns and counties. E. g. Whitney, Peter. History of the County of Worcester. Worcester (Mass.). 1793.

[2] These were Boston, 33,250; Salem, 12,600; and Providence, 10,000.

[3] For fuller statement of these figures see Appendix A.

[4] There were 16 towns along the Connecticut River from Saybrook to Springfield, only two of which had less than 2,500 people.

[5] Both of these towns contained about 70 square miles and profited besides by their location in the Connecticut Valley.

them off more or less distinctly from the small number of larger towns and so justify the classification.

The Villages.

A part of the inhabitants of the inland towns lived in villages, small groups of houses often surrounding the meeting house on the top of a hill in the center of the town, or lying stretched out along a single broad street, or enclosing an open square at the intersection of two highways; the remainder lived in farm-houses scattered over the area of the town outside the village. It was these village settlements which, as President Dwight so clearly pointed out,[1] distinguished southern New England from the Southern states as well as from the frontier regions of the northern parts of New England and from the new communities in the Western states. Resulting originally from a need of protection from the hostile natives and also from the desire to have dwellings convenient to the place of religious worship, these villages became a traditional part of New England life and served to foster the growth of a communal spirit. They made possible compulsory education of children and in general prevented the degeneration in manners and morals which inevitably follows as a consequence of dispersion of people in a new country.[2]

From the point of view of the economic life of the inhabitants, however, these villages were not significant. In the first place, they were not large enough to include any very great proportion of the entire population, and, besides, the occupations of the village dwellers were essentially the same as those of their fellow-townsmen. As regards the size of these villages, contemporary writers have given us an abundance of information. In 1781 Chastellux referred to Lebanon, Conn., as one of the most considerable towns, *i.e.*, villages, in the country (in the rural inland region.) It had 100 houses which were somewhat scattered.[3] The same writer found 50 houses around

[1] Dwight, Timothy. Travels in New England and New York. 4 vols. London. 1823. I. 300–303.

[2] The importance of the services rendered by the country churches in furnishing a social center can hardly be over-emphasized. A clear statement of the nature of these services is found in Adams, Charles Francis. Three Episodes in Massachusetts History. A Study in Church and Town Government. 2 vols. Boston. 1892. II. 750–751.

[3] Chastellux, François Jean, Marquis de. Travels in North America. 2 vols. London. 1788. I. 455. Another French traveler who passed through this town a few years later found 150–160 houses in the village. See La Rochefoucauld-Liancourt, Duc de. Travels through the United States of North America. 2 vols. London. 1799. I. 515.

a large square in Litchfield, Conn.; about the same number collected about a meeting-house in Farmington; in Windham, also in
this state, some 40 or 50 houses were seen "pretty near each other,"
forming a square.[1]   The same type of village was seen by Professor
Silliman in Lenox, Mass.   It had 100 houses gathered about three
churches, an academy and a courthouse.[2]   Killingworth, Conn.,
furnished an example of what might be called an "extended village."
On its broad main street, six rods wide and one and one-half miles
long, were 65 houses.   In another part of the town there was a village of 109 houses.[3]   From a general survey of such figures as are
given in Pease and Niles' Gazetteer it seems that in the great majority of towns the villages contained less than 50 houses.[4]

Occupations of the Village-Dwellers.

An examination of the distribution of land ownership in the inland towns shows that the occupations of the dwellers in these minute
nuclei of population, the villages, did not differ essentially from those
of their neighbors who lived on scattered farms along the country
roads.   They were all farmers.   In describing the type of village
found in the Connecticut Valley, President Dwight says: "The
town plat is originally distributed into lots containing from two to
ten acres.   In a convenient spot, on each of these, a house is erected
at the bottom of the courtyard (often neatly enclosed); and is furnished universally with a barn, and other convenient outbuildings.
. . . . The lot, on which the house stands, universally styled
the home lot, is almost of course a meadow, richly cultivated, covered during the pleasant season with verdure, and containing generally a thrifty orchard."[5]   Besides these home lots the village dwellers

[1] Chastellux.   Op. cit., I. 48, 38, 23.
[2] Silliman, Benjamin.   Remarks on a Short Tour between Hartford and Quebec.   New Haven. 1820. p. 39.
[3] See Field, D. D.   A Statistical Account of the County of Middlesex in Connecticut.   Published by the Connecticut Academy of the Arts and Sciences.
Middletown. 1819. pp. 108–109.
[4] Taking 12 towns from various counties in Connecticut, we find the following numbers of houses collected in villages: Litchfield, 84; Harwinton, 15–20;
Plymouth, 20; Hampton, 20; Farmington, 100; Newtown, 50–60; Milford, 100;
Brooklyn, 20; Sterling, 30; Voluntown, 15; Tolland, 30; East Windsor, 40.   Of
these towns Litchfield and Farmington were exceptionally large both in area
and population, and Milford was situated on the coast, affording its inhabitants
opportunity for maritime occupations.
[5] Travels, II. 317.   For a more general description of the New England villages see Lambert, John.   Travels in Lower Canada and North America.   London. 1810. 2 vols. II. 307–308, and Duncan, John M.   Travels through the
United States and Canada.   2 vols. New York. 1823. I. 94–95.

had outlying fields, which had been apportioned to the heads of the families at the original settlement of the town.[1] On both these tracts they carried on agricultural operations in the same manner and to the same extent as did the farmers outside the village. The only difference between the two types of farmers seems to have been that the village dwellers were at a considerable disadvantage in going back and forth from their houses to their fields.[2]

Ministers, Lawyers and Physicians.

There were, however, of necessity, some persons in the town who had other interests besides agriculture, and these generally lived in the village. In the first place, there were always a few representatives of what we now call the professional class. At least one clergyman, one lawyer and one physician were evidently indispensable to each community. Of these, the minister seems to have been the one whose "calling" was most sharply distinguished from agriculture. President Dwight takes especial pains to deny the generally accepted report that the country ministers worked on their farms, except in the newest settlements.[3] The ministers lived on farms, however, and drew from them a considerable addition to their meager salaries.[4] The accounts of the settlement of new towns tell of the reservation of a certain share of the land for the minister, in clearing which he was assisted by his parishioners.[5] There was

[1] For a description of the method of apportioning land in early New England towns, see Weeden, William B. Economic and Social History of New England, 1620–1789. 2 vols. Boston. 1890. I. 53–62 and II. 512–515. Also Maclear, Anne B. Early New England Towns. New York. 1908. pp. 81–101, and Andrews, Charles M. The River Towns of Connecticut. In Johns Hopkins University Studies in History and Political Science. 7th series, VII–VIII–IX. pp. 32–79.

[2] See Porter, Noah. Historical Discourse Delivered before the Citizens of Farmington (Conn.). Hartford. 1841. Appendix. Note S. p. 83.

[3] Travels, IV. 436. On the other hand, we have occasional references to the activity of ministers as farmers, as in Warville, Brissot de. New Travels in the United States of America. London. 1792. p. 453.

[4] According to MacMaster, History of the People of the United States, 6 vols., New York. 1885–1913, II. 568, the salaries of country ministers at this time varied from £75 to £140. The New England pound being equal to $3.33, this would make them worth from $250 to $550. At a somewhat later date the salaries of ministers in Middlesex County, Conn., varied from $230 to $1000. In addition to the salary a settlement of from £100 to £200, payable either in currency or in kind, was made on the installation of a new pastor. Field, Statistical Account. p. 145.

[5] See Belknap, Jeremy. History of New Hampshire. 3 vols. Boston. 1792. III. 324.

a tendency as land grew more valuable and as the ability of the parishioners to pay a salary, either in currency or in kind, also increased, for the parishes to dispose of their land holdings. But in 1810 much remained,[1] and even now in rural towns the parsonages are often situated on small farms. Although the clergymen were not farmers in the same sense or on the same scale as their parishioners, yet cultivating a kitchen garden and keeping a cow or two and some small stock were occupations which furnished some part of their living and, moreover, were not inconsistent with clerical dignity.

Lawyers and physicians appear regularly in every account of village life of this period. Scarcely any town managed to get along without at least one lawyer and a couple of "doctors."[2] Travelers remarked on the importance of the legal profession in southern New England, especially in Connecticut, and attributed the fact to the litigious spirit of the people.[3] It may be, however, that other more rational causes can be found. As a matter of fact, this profession offered practically the only opportunity for an ambitious young man to bring himself into prominence in the world which lay outside his own community. As a country doctor or minister he might live and die unheard of beyond the circle of a few towns, but with only the smattering of a legal education he might become a justice of the peace, a selectman, and finally be sent to the state legislature. From that vantage-ground his talents, whatever they might be, would have at least a chance to display themselves. An examination of the careers of the men who were most prominent in the politics of southern New England at the beginning of the century shows in fact that a large proportion of them had been country

---

[1] See Field. Statistical Account, 145–148.

[2] A compilation of the statistics given in Pease and Niles' Gazetteer gives the following result for two typical counties in Connecticut:

	No. of Towns	Lawyers	Physicians
Windham.............................	13	24	44
Tolland..................................	11	14	27

In four towns in Windham County the lawyers were lacking but in the town of Windham, where the county court was held, there were eight. In this county there were five towns which had each four or more physicians.

[3] See Harriott, Lieut. John. Struggles Through Life. London. 1807. II. 55. Wansey, the English clothier, tells us that the best houses in Connecticut were inhabited by lawyers. Journal of an Excursion to the United States of America. Salisbury (England). 1796. p. 70.

lawyers.[1] While waiting for political preferment, or in the intervals between terms of office, the country lawyer would have had a hard time to make a living if he had relied on his legal work alone. Consequently, he sometimes took up a trade such as that of carpenter or shoemaker,[2] but most often made up the deficiencies in his income by farming.[3]

This partial reliance upon agriculture was equally true of the medical profession. They were, in many cases, men with a smattering of knowledge concerning the effect of certain drugs and herbs on the most common diseases,—primarily farmers, who, as Miss Larned says of the doctors in Canterbury, practiced medicine when they had nothing more important to do.[4] The inventory of the estate of a physician of that region shows to what extent he had combined the two occupations. Besides a stock of drugs, medicines and vials, he had one pair of oxen, 13 cows, 15 head of young cattle, 20 sheep, a number of swine, farming tools, hay, etc. It was probably the fact that much of the medical service of the time was being done by poorly educated men who were farmers as well, which caused so much complaint to be made of the inefficiency of the profession at that time.[5]

The Business Men.

Besides these professional men, there were in the rural villages a small group of men who represented in a way the prototype of what we now call the class of business men. There was the taverner or innkeeper, the country trader, the proprietors of the saw-mills,

---

[1] Taking a list of 64 prominent men at this time, including governors, United States Senators and state officials and legislators, whose previous occupation can be ascertained, we find that 36 of these had been lawyers, 13 were merchants, 10 had come into prominence during the Revolution, 3 were physicians, and 2 were craftsmen. Examples of men of prominence who were originally lawyers in country towns are furnished by Uriah Tracy, United States Senator from Connecticut, Jonathan Trumbull, the elder, Governor of Connecticut, and Caleb Strong, Governor of Massachusetts.

[2] See Neilsen, Peter. Recollections of a Six Years Residence in the United States of America. Glasgow. 1830. p. 182.

[3] Advertisements in the country newspapers such as that in the Massachusetts Spy, published in the town of Worcester, issue of July 1, 1807, are good evidence on this point. This advertisement recommends a farm of 23 acres which is offered for sale as a suitable purchase for a lawyer.

[4] Larned, Ellen Douglas. History of Windham County, Conn., 2 vols. Worcester (Mass.). 1874–1880. II. 423.

[5] See La Rochefoucauld-Liancourt, Travels, I. 448, and Neilson, Recollections, pp. 188–189.

the grist-mills, the fulling-mills, the tanneries; the village artisans or mechanics, the blacksmiths, the carpenters and joiners, and the cobblers. In a mere numerical consideration these occupations might seem to have formed an important element in the economic life of the community, but, on closer observation, it becomes evident that these, too, were usually only auxillary occupations, by-industries of agriculture.

The New England tavern served a wide variety of purposes and its proprietor must needs be a man of varied talents. If situated on a stage-coach route it provided the clean beds and the wholesome fare which were so much appreciated by travelers.[1] Far more important were its services to the townsfolk as a common gathering-place. As a social center it rivaled the meeting-house to whose moral atmosphere it presented a decided contrast. Here much of the political business of the town was transacted; the selectmen's meetings and the sessions of the town court were held regularly in its main room; and at times, in winter, when the meeting-house was too cold, the town meetings held an adjourned session there. It was the scene of many village festivities; the singing school and the dancing school, where the liberal tone of the community permitted such frivolity, met there; on muster days the tavern was the headquarters of the train band. On most of these occasions the tavern bar, where strong liquors were dispensed, was liberally patronized. This feature, too, proved a strong attraction for the village topers and ne'er-do-wells.[2] It was this multiplicity of services to the community rather than the patronage of the infrequent travelers which explains the uniform occurrence of taverns in inland towns. They were, of course, most numerous on the post-roads between New York and Boston, but even in the smallest and most isolated towns at least one tavern could usually be found.[3]

[1] Brissot de Warville discusses appreciatively an inn in Spencer, Mass. Travels, I. 124.

[2] See Field, Edward. The Colonial Tavern. Providence. 1897. Also Mac-Master, History of the United States. II. 564–565. Adams, C. F. Episodes, II. 783.

[3] Chastellux, Travels, I. 50, while traveling in Connecticut, writes of a law which requires public houses at intervals of every six miles on the great roads. Such a law, however, does not appear in the statutes in force in the three states of southern New England at the end of the eighteenth century. In Massachusetts and Connecticut, the local authorities were invested with power to determine the number of taverns deemed necessary in each town, and to appoint fit persons as keepers. The latter were required to give bonds and pay a license fee. Connecticut Pub-

The tavern-keeper was a versatile individual. "He led the singing in the meeting house on Sunday; ran the ferry if his tavern was
situated near a stream; acted as schoolmaster for the children of
those who frequented his house; served his fellow men in the legislature, town council, selectmen, and other minor offices; ruled with
solemn dignity over the local courts; headed the Train Band on training or squadron days; kept order in the meeting house on Sundays;
surveyed the lands assigned to the land-crazy townsmen; . . .
and in fact, next to the town clerk, was the most important and learned
man in the place."[1] Besides these possible lines of activity, he was
often a physician, and usually owned and managed a farm from
the produce of which he supplied a part at least of the wants of
his patrons.[2]

The Country Store.

The country store was as regularly found in New England towns
as the tavern; in some cases the two institutions were combined
in the same building, under the same proprietorship. In the typical inland town there were generally not more than two stores and,
in many cases, only one.[3] The stock in trade was regularly described in their advertisements as European and West India goods.

lic Statute Laws. I. 640–645. 1808, and Massachusetts Perpetual Laws. pp.
55–63. 1788. License fees were also demanded in Rhode Island, although the
regulations were in general less strict in this state.   Rhode Island Public Laws.
Revision of 1798, pp. 393–394, 580.

[1] See Field, Edward. The Colonial Tavern. pp. 41–42.

[2] Advertisements of farms for sale in the country newspapers clearly demon-
strate this fact. See Massachusetts Spy, Jan. 28, June 22, 1807, and National
Aegis (Worcester, Mass.), April 25, 1804. Another fact which shows the close
relation between this business and the usual occupations of the agricultural population, was the practice of "laying oneself out to give entertainment." In outlying districts where the taverns were either bad or inconveniently situated, or
perhaps entirely lacking, a traveler often applied for food and lodging to any
"householder of substance," who was not unwilling to accept a moderate sum
in return. President Dwight was often accommodated in this way, especially
in the northern states of New England. See also Kendall, Edward Augustus.
Travels through the Northern Parts of the United States. New York. 1809.
3 vols. II. 147; and Kittredge. George Lyman. The Old Farmer and his Almanack. Boston. 1904. pp. 282–283.

[3] The descriptions of the various towns given by Whitney in his History of
Worcester County, Mass., show that the usual number of stores was two in each
town. The advertisements in the newspapers published in inland towns such
as Leominster, Stockbridge, and Brookfield, Massachusetts, rarely contain
notice of more than one country store.

Under the first of these euphonious phrases were included a few pieces of imported dress-goods, crockery, glassware, powder and shot, and bars of iron and steel. The West India goods were salt, molasses, rum and other liquors, indigo, spices and sugar.[1] In regions of active internal trade, where the farm produce could find outlet to a market, as for instance in the towns along the Connecticut River,[2] or in the southern part of Windham County, Conn.,[3] the country traders were numerous and did a brisk business. They bought up dairy products and salted pork and beef as well as household manufactures from the farmers and undertook, on their own responsibility, often, the sale of these products in the Southern states or in the West Indies. In the isolated rural community, however, business must have been extremely dull. Some profit could be made from the exchange of goods among the members of the community; but of goods from the outside the latter were able to purchase very little. Some salt and a few other necessary articles they had to have; the liquors they often bought in preference to the things which they really needed and were often largely in debt to the storekeeper on this account.[4] In order to eke out a living the storekeeper resorted to agriculture, either tilling the land himself or hiring occasional assistance from his neighbors.[5]

[1] An unusually detailed advertisement is that of a Worcester, Mass., merchant who has to sell: West India goods and groceries, viz: Best cognac and Spanish brandy; West India and New England rums; real Holland gin; Madeira wines; flour, molasses; loaf, white and brown sugar; teas, coffee, chocolate, spices, raisins, copperas; alum; rock and fine salt; dried and pickled fish; glazed china tea sets, crockery and glass ware, violins and flutes. He offers to give cash for country produce. National Aegis, November 20, 1804.

[2] A very great difference is observable between the character of the advertisements in newspapers published in the river towns such as Middletown, Hartford, Springfield, Northampton, and Greenfield and those published in the towns mentioned in Note 3, p. 258.

[3] See Windham Herald, 1808. Larned, History of Windham County, II. 426.

[4] Mr. Adams seems to be justified in his opinion that the sale of liquors was a large part of the business of the country store. He says: "In every store in which West India goods were sold, and there were no others, behind the counter stood the casks of Jamaica and New England rum, of gin and brandy. Their contents were sold by the gallon, the bottle or the glass. They were carried away or drunk on the spot." Episodes. II. 790.

[5] As witness the advertisements in country newspapers. Such an advertisement is that found in the National Aegis of a farm of 90 acres in the town of Paxon, Worcester County, Mass., on which is a combined store and tavern. April 25, 1804.

Village Industries.

Every town had its complement of grist-mills, saw-mills and fulling-mills; usually there were three or four of the grist and saw-mills and one or two fulling-mills.[1] The grist-mills ground the farmer's corn and rye; the saw-mill prepared the lumber for building purposes; the fulling-mill, or clothier's works, as it was sometimes called, contained simple machinery for shrinking and dressing the cloth which had been spun and woven in the farm-houses.[2] Combined with the fulling-mill was often a carding machine which performed by water power the laborious operations of preparing the wool for spinning. These machines had only recently been introduced,[3] but had spread so rapidly that by 1810 they were found in almost every town. The business carried on by these mills was often interrupted in summer by the failure of the streams on which they depended for their water power; at other times it was small in amount, being limited almost without exception to the needs of the community.[4] The number of mills in a community is by no means an indication of an equal number of proprietors receiving their entire income from this sort of industrial activity. Often various sorts of mills were carried on under one ownership, and besides the proprietors of these various enterprises were regularly farmers as well.[5]

[1] Exceptionally large towns such as Litchfield, in Connecticut, had a much larger number of these mills.

[2] The business of a fulling-mill in Cheshire County, N. H., is described in detail in Gallatin's Report on Manufactures, American State Papers, Finance, II. 435. Its labor force consisted of two men and four apprentices, working four months in the year. The total amount of cloth dressed was 6,700 yards per annum. Such mills were often erroneously designated as woolen factories in early descriptions of manufactures.

[3] About 1800.

[4] An exception is found in the case of towns within reach of a market, as for example the coast towns of Fairfield County, Conn., in which considerable milling of flour was done.

[5] An instance is given by Miss Larned in her History of Windham County. In Pomfret, Conn., in 1787, one Captain Cargill owned and operated three sets of grist-mills, a bolting-mill, a blacksmith's shop, a fulling mill, and a churning mill, all on the same water power and under the same roof. Vol. II. p. 266. See also Ibid. II. 240.

An illustration of the combination of several of these enterprises with farming is given in the Hampshire Gazette (Northampton, Mass.), Feb. 20, 1811. A farm of 130 acres is advertised in the town of Savoy, having on the premises a store, potash works, grist-mill, and saw-mill. As if these were not enough to keep the future owner busy, the seller adds that the place is a good site for a tavern.

A tannery or two.seem to have been uniformly a part of the economic outfit of the inland town.[1] The working dress of the people was largely composed of leathern garments, not only their shoes and leggings, but shirts, breeches and coats as well. A large part of the material came from the hides of animals slaughtered on the farms and prepared at the village tannery. This was a primitive affair, quite on a par with the mills in the size of its plant and in the scope of its operations.[2] Cider mills and cider and grain distilleries were numerous, but were for the most part owned by farmers and located on their premises.[3]

The manufacture of potash and pearl ash was a by-industry of the farmers in many towns, especially in newly settled regions in Vermont and New Hampshire, and in Worcester and Berkshire counties in Massachusetts. La Rochefoucauld described the process of preparing potash "which is generally observed in the United States," as follows: "Large tubs, with a double bottom, are filled with ashes; the uppermost bottom which contains several holes, is covered with ashes, about ten or eleven inches deep, while the under part of the tub is filled with straw or hay. Water, being poured over the ashes, extracts the particles of salt, and discharges all the heterogeneous matter which it may contain in the layer of hay or straw. The lie is drawn off by means of a cock, and if it should not yet have attained a sufficient degree of strength, poured again over the ashes. The lie is deemed sufficiently strong when an egg swims on it. This lie is afterward boiled in large iron cauldrons, which are constantly filled out of other cauldrons, in which lie is likewise boiling . . . . This salt is of a black colour, and called *black potash.* Some manufacturers leave the potash in this state in the cauldron,

[1] In the state of Connecticut, for instance, according to the Digest of Manufactures prepared by Tench Coxe from the facts collected in the Census of 1810, there were 408 tanneries. An examination of Pease and Niles' Gazetteer shows that these establishments were scattered fairly evenly among the 119 towns.

[2] An early tannery in the town of Quincy, Mass., is described by Mr. Adams as follows: "The earlier tanneries were strange primitive establishments. The vats were oblong boxes sunk in the ground close to the edge of the town brook at the point where it crossed the main street. They were without either covers or outlets. The beam-house was an open shed, within which old, worn-out, horses circulated round while the bark was crushed at the rate of half a cord or so a day by alternate wooden and stone wheels, moving in a circular trough fifteen feet in diameter." Episodes, II. 929.

[3] Coxe, Tench. A View of the United States of America. London. 1794. p. 269. The manufacture of cider brandy was an important by-industry of the farmers of Woodbury, Conn. Pease and Niles, Gazetteer, p. 267.

and encrease the fire, by means of which the oil is disengaged from
the salt in a thick smoke, and the black potash assumes a grey colour,
in which state it is packed up in barrels for sale.

* * * * * * * * * * *

Pearlash is potash purified by calcination. To this end the potash is put into a kiln, constructed in oval form, of Plaster of Paris;
the inside of which being made otherwise perfectly close, is hori-
zontally intersected by an iron grate, on which the potash is placed.
Under this grate a fire is made, and the heat, reverberated from the
arched upper part of the kiln, compleats the calcination, and con-
verts the potash into pearlash; . . . . The process of calcination lasts about an hour."[1]

The apparatus necessary for this manufacture was inexpensive,
the largest outlay being for the purchase of the kettles in which
the lye was boiled. The products, pearlash and potash, were used
to some extent in the household in making soap, in scouring wool,
and in bleaching and dyeing cloth. The larger part of the output
was sold, partly for use in glass-making and other manufactures,
and partly for export.

The Mechanics and Artisans.

We have next to consider the country mechanics or artisans.
Here we find that although the division of labor seems to have progressed to a considerable degree in the separation of crafts, yet the
connection of each with the fundamental industry, that of tilling the
soil, was as close and as rarely completely dissolved as in the case
of the professional or business men already described. This imperfect specialization of occupations is described by Tench Coxe
as follows: "Those of the tradesmen and manufacturers, who live
in the country, generally reside on small lots and farms, from one
acre to twenty; and not a few upon farms from twenty to one hundred and fifty acres; which they cultivate at leisure times, with their
own hands, their wives, children, servants, and apprentices, and
sometimes by hired labourers, or by letting out fields, for a part
of the produce, to some neighbour, who has time or farm hands
not fully employed. *This union of manufactures and farming*[2] is
found to be very convenient on the grain farms; but it is still more

---

[1] Rochefoucauld-Liancourt, Travels, I. 384–386. See also Bishop, J. Leander.
History of American Manufactures. 2 vols. Philadelphia. 1861. II. 57.

[2] Author's italics.

convenient on the grazing and grass farms, where parts of almost every day, and a great part of the year, can be spared from the business of the farm, and employed in some mechanical, handycraft, or manufacturing business. These persons often make domestic and farming carriages, implements, and utensils, build houses, tan leather, and manufacture hats, shoes, hosiery, cabinet-work, and other articles of clothing and furniture, to the great convenience and advantage of the neighbourhood. In like manner some of the farmers, at leisure times and proper seasons, manufacture nails, pot-ash, pearl-ash, staves and heading, hoops and handspikes, axe-handles, maple-sugar, &c."[1]

Further testimony on this point is given by Brissot de Warville,[2] who says of the region of Worcester County, Mass.: "Almost all these houses are inhabited by men who are both cultivators and arti-zans; one is a tanner, another a shoemaker, another sells goods; but all are farmers." If we seek for confirmatory evidence from the size of farms or the amount of land held by these artisans, a serious difficulty arises. They naturally tended to congregate in the small village settlements, where customers would have ready access to them. The gazetteers often speak of the "mechanics' shops" in their descriptions of these villages.[3] These shops were located in or near the dwellings on the "home lots." Consequently, when we find advertisements of such shops for sale with amounts of land varying from one to ten acres,[4] we are not justified in concluding that these men could not be farmers; for, as we have seen, large outlying fields were as a rule held by all village dwellers, and the home lots held by the artizans correspond in extent with those held by men who were purely and simply farmers.

When we consider the numbers of the craftsmen in the various trades both separately and as a body, in proportion to the popula-tion of towns in which they worked, our conclusion of their partial dependence on agriculture is still further strengthened. Fortunately we have complete lists of the artisans in two typical rural towns in Litchfield County, Conn., one (Cornwall) of 1600 population and the other (Washington) having 1575. They are as follows:

[1] In his View of the United States, pp. 442–443.
[2] Travels, I. 127.
[3] Pease and Niles, Gazetteer, pp. 183–184. Art. New Fairfield, Conn.
[4] Such advertisements are to be found in the Massachusetts Spy, Feb. 28, Oct. 14, and 19, 1807; National Aegis, Oct. 26, 1807. Also in the Windham Herald and other newspapers published in small inland towns. Occasionally instances of farms of 50–70 acres with shops are found.

	CORNWALL	WASHINGTON
Shoemakers...	20	11
Carpenters...	4	8
Blacksmiths..	7	8
Tailors..	5	4
Coopers...	6	7
Carriage and wagon makers........................	3	4
Cabinet and chair makers..........................	2	2
Saddlers...	0	1
Total..	47	45[1]

It would be impossible, on account of changed habits of consumption and on account of the great quantities of articles manufactured for a wide market which are bought and sold in a modern city, to make any valuable comparison between the present ratio of craftsmen to the total population with that found in 1810. Such a comparison, however, may be made between conditions existing in these rural communities and in Hartford, Conn., in 1819, as described by Pease and Niles. In a population of 6,901 (1820), this city had the following craftsmen:

Housejoiners and carpenters.....................................	19
Shoemakers..	15
Blacksmiths...	13
Coopers...	10
Cabinet and chair makers......................................	8

[1] The statistics for Cornwall are taken from Pease and Niles, Gazetteer, pp 244–245, and those for Washington from Morris, James A. Statistical Account of Several Towns in the County of Litchfield. Published by the Connecticut Academy of the Arts and Sciences. Vol. I. New Haven. 1811.

An interesting table of the same sort appears in the description of Middlebury, Vt., in the Massachusetts Historical Society's collections, Series II. Vol. 9. p. 131. It had in 1820 in a population of about 2300 (Census figures for 1820 do not give population by towns in Vermont) the following artisans: Hatters, 3; shoemakers, 8; tailors, 3; milliners, 4; saddlers, 3; goldsmiths, 2; blacksmiths, 9; gunsmiths, 1; glaziers, 1; wheelwrights, 5; painters, 1; coopers, 2; tinners, 2; potters, 4; tanners, 3; bakers, 2; cabinetmakers, 3; housejoiners, 14; masons, 6; and in addition 4 saw-mills, 1 oil mill, 1 paper mill and 2 potash works.

Tench Coxe, in his View of the United States, pp. 312–313, gives a list of the artisans in Lancaster, Penn., the largest inland town in the United States in 1790 (population ca. 3500). It had 234 craftsmen of the most diverse sorts. Lists are also given for four other inland towns, Washington, Pittsburgh, Bedford and Huntington. Ibid. p. 311.

Tailors... 11
Carriage makers and wheelwrights........................... 6
Master masons... 6
Butchers... 16
Painters... 6
Leather workers... 2
Hatters... 2[1]

If we may assume that in Hartford these were specialized artisans, devoting their whole time to the practice of their trades and producing only for the local market,[2] then we may from these figures establish normal ratios of the various types of craftsmen to the total population. The comparison of these ratios with those shown by the statistics of Cornwall and Washington is striking. In only

	CORNWALL	WASHINGTON	HARTFORD
Shoemakers........................	1 to 80	1 to 143	1 to 258
Carpenters........................	1 to 400	1 to 197	1 to 460
Tailors............................	1 to 220	1 to 395	1 to 630
Blacksmiths.......................	1 to 229	1 to 197	1 to 530
Coopers...........................	1 to 267	1 to 225	1 to 690
Carriage makers....................	1 to 534	1 to 394	1 to 1150
Cabinet makers.....................	1 to 800	1 to 788	1 to 850
Leather workers....................		1 to 1575	1 to 3450

one case, that of the carpenters, is there evidence of greater specialization on the part of the rural craftsmen. In general we find them serving a much narrower market than their colleagues in the city. Compare the position of the shoemakers in the country and in the city. We find them making shoes for from three to nine times as many people in the city as in the country; the tailor and the blacksmith in the city both have about twice as many customers as their colleagues in the country towns. To my mind, these figures are the strongest sort of corroborative evidence in support of such a general statement as that of Tench Coxe.[3] It seems clear that the 40 to 50 artisans found in a rural town were not representatives of a specialized class in industry, but rather were farmers who had acquired

[1] Pease and Niles, Gazetteer, p. 43.
[2] Although there is no direct evidence on these points, yet the general descriptions given in the gazetteers of this city and of towns of this size seem to justify the assumption. Certainly there is no evidence showing that craftsmen in such a city sold any of their products to a wide market.
[3] Quoted on pages 262-263.

skill in some particular trade, putting it to advantage in the dull seasons of their principal occupation, by doing odd jobs for their neighbors. Certainly making the shoes needed by sixteen or even thirty families, or building and repairing houses for forty or eighty families would have been insufficient occupation for the head of a family. Only by this combination of occupations, "this union of manufactures and farming," as Tench Coxe called it, could they have existed.[1]

The Lack of Division of Labor—Causes and Results.

This completes the survey of the various occupations of the inhabitants and the analysis of the extent of the division of labor in the inland town. We may summarize the results as follows: In the first place, an examination of the method of settlement in the villages, those diminutive points of concentration of the rural population, showed that their inhabitants were farmers—producers and not merely consumers of food stuffs. Then, taking up successively the representatives of what we now call the professional class, the business men and the artisans, or country mechanics, we reached the same conclusion in regard to each, viz.; that with the usual exception of the minister, all of these 50 to 60 men[2] held farms which provided their food as well as other necessities of life.[3] We may think, then, of this whole group of persons as standing on the borderline between agriculture and a specialized non-agricultural occupation. They were at times doctors, lawyers, innkeepers or storekeepers, fullers, carpenters, or tanners, but most of the time plain farmers.

[1] This class of country mechanics offers many interesting points of comparison with and contrast to the "Lohnwerker" described by Bücher in his "Entstehung der Volkswirtschaft." 9 Aufl. pp. 170–171. The "Störer" or itinerant workers which he describes there had their counterpart in the traveling weavers, tailors, and cobblers who worked up the raw material of the farmers into finished goods on the spot. See Earle, Alice Morse. Home Life in Colonial Days. New York. 1898. pp. 212–213; and Larned, History of Windham County, II. 395.
   The blacksmith, the most indispensable of all the rural artisans, was perhaps also the most regularly employed of all. Yet very often, up to within recent years, he also has been a farmer. The variety of products turned out in a smith's shop may be learned from the account books of Hezekiah Bunnell which are preserved in the library of the New Haven Historical Society. They cover the years 1725–1764, during which he carried on his business in West Haven, Cheshire and Farmington, Conn. They also illustrate the fact that the payment for the services of the artisans was often in kind.
[2] In a typical town, say of 1500 to 2000 persons.
[3] For a description of various industries carried on in farm houses see infra, Chapter VI.

Thus we can see that the distinction between various occupations which we had set up for purposes of analysis tends to vanish. The broad outlines of a future division of employments were marked out, but the process of separation was as yet hardly begun.

The disadvantages of this lack of specialization, this combination of several professions, occupations or trades in each individual, are obvious and must have been recognized even then. The doctor and the lawyer, the cobbler and the carpenter, as well as the community which they served, must have known that each one of them could have been far more efficient if only he could have devoted his entire attention to one occupation. They knew "practice makes perfect," and how could the practice of any trade or profession be-become perfect when it must continually be interrupted in order to procure from the soil a partial subsistence? If they recognized the defects in their economic organization, why did they not remedy them? If they realized the advantages which might be expected from greater specialization, why did they not introduce it? The solution of this problem is found in the limited extent of the demand for the services of the non-agricultural class. The towns were small and the purchasing power of the farmers, for reasons which will appear in later chapters, was set within very narrow limits. Hence such a community could not furnish sufficient demand for the products and services of specialized non-agricultural workers to provide the latter with a living. Their only resource to supply the deficiency in income was the soil. Hence the union of all trades, businesses and professions with agriculture.[1]

Our interest in this essay is primarily in the agricultural population; hence it is pertinent to inquire how the farmers were affected by this combination of employments which we have observed in the rural town. Did it make any difference to the plain farmer, the man who was getting his living merely from cultivating the soil, whether his neighbors, the miller and the carpenter, were farmers

---

[1] No better illustration than this could be desired of the famous dictum of Adam Smith that "the division of labour is limited by the extent of the market." He says: "As it is the power of exchanging that gives occasion to the division of labour, so the extent of this division must always be limited by the extent of that power, or, in other words, by the extent of the market. When the market is very small, no person can have any encouragement to dedicate himself entirely to one employment, for want of the power to exchange all that surplus part of the produce of his own labour, which is over and above his consumption, for such parts of the produce of other men's labour as he has occasion for." *Wealth of Nations.* Book I. Chap. III. p. 15. (Everyman's edition).

as well as craftsmen? Obviously, the practice of agriculture by all the members of the community meant that none of them could have an opportunity to sell anything regularly to his neighbors. That is, under such conditions as we have described, there was no market for agricultural produce in the inland town. What this state of affairs meant to the farmers and how far it determined the character of the agricultural industry, and of home and community life, are subjects which are best considered in later chapters.

Manufactures in Inland Towns.

The question naturally arises at this point, How far were such communities as these described typical of all the towns in southern New England? Were there not, perhaps, some towns in which manufacturing or commercial enterprises had concentrated an industrial or a maritime population? And, if so, to what extent did these furnish a demand for the farmers' produce?

A casual survey of the list of articles manufactured in the Northern and Eastern states as reported in the official statements of Hamilton (1791),[1] Gallatin (1810),[2] and Coxe (1814)[3] would lead one to expect that somewhere in these states a considerable concentration of industrial workers might be found. Among the articles there enumerated were soap and candles, tallow and spermaceti; leather goods, linen, cotton and woolen cloth, cabinet ware and furniture, hats, paper, spirituous and malted liquors, cordage, manufactures of iron, gunpowder, glass and earthenware. But when we come to analyze the methods by which these articles were produced it becomes evident that only a few of them were, in any significant sense of the word, manufactures. The great majority of the articles included under this term were produced either in the household, as for instance a large part of the soap and candles, woolen and linen cloth, or in craftsmen's shops, as were the furniture and the leather goods. Such goods were either consumed in the family which produced them or disposed of within the community. Of these articles there was practically nothing produced for a wide market, and consequently there was no cause for the growth of an industrial population. In the case of such articles as cordage, liquors, gunpowder and glass there was real manufacturing. But this was carried on for the most part in a few coast towns, such as Boston, Norwich, Providence and

[1] American State Papers, Finance, I. 123.
[2] Ibid. II. 425–439.
[3] Ibid. II. 666–677.

New Haven, and the effect which these enterprises may have had in creating a market for farm produce is best considered in connection with the commercial activities of these towns.

In many inland towns, it is true, there were enterprises already established producing small articles of various sorts which were disposed of in a market much wider than that of the local community. Such were the buttons, tinware,[1] clocks, combs, and other "Yankee notions" which formed the stock in trade of the peddlers in their annual trips to the Southern states. Yet the production of these articles was conducted on such a minute scale, at this early date, that no noticeable concentration of an industrial population resulted. Towns like Waterbury, or Plymouth, or Berlin, in Connecticut, or Leominster in Massachusetts,[2] were not noticeably different, in the opening years of the century, from the hundreds of other inland towns which had no manufacturing enterprises. Their population was not larger than that of many prosperous agricultural towns[3] and the presence in them of ten or a dozen industrial workers would not have meant much to the farmers. Besides the articles enumerated above, some towns made paper, some linseed oil,[4] others earthenware and pottery[5] in establishments or mills of much the same sort as the grist-mills and saw-mills which were regular features of the village economy.

Hats.

There were only a few branches of manufacture, some carried on in inland and others in coast towns, which had become sufficiently

---

[1] For a description of the tinware industry in Berlin and of the methods of marketing this and other small manufactures see Dwight, Travels, II. 43–45. Also Kendall, Travels, I. 128–129. A consideration of the early development of many small manufactures in Connecticut towns, including tinware, clocks and buttons, will be found in Lathrop, William G. The Brass Industry in Connecticut. New Haven. 1909.

[2] In Leominster 6500 dozen combs were produced annually by a labor force varying from ten to twenty men. See Whitney, History of the County of Worcester, p. 198.

[3] In 1810 the populations of Waterbury and Berlin were 2900 each; Plymouth, where clocks were made in a few small shops, had 1900 people and Leominister 1600.

[4] According to the statistics collected for the census of 1810 there were 19 paper mills and 24 oil mills in Connecticut, 22 oil mills and 33 paper mills in Massachusetts, and 3 of each sort in Rhode Island.

[5] See Larned, History of Windham, II. 365. These goods were also marketed by peddlers.

important to deserve especial consideration. The manufacture of fur and woolen hats, which in many inland towns was carried on in small shops for a purely local market, had in Fairfield County, Connecticut, been developed into an export industry. In 1810 the census credited this county with a product of 350,000 hats. Most of these were made in the town of Danbury, where there were 56 hat shops employing from three to five men each.[1] As a result of the growth of this industry the population of the town had increased from 3,180 to 3,600 in the decade 1800–1810. Hats were also manufactured in smaller quantities in New London.[2]

The Iron Industry.

Iron furnaces, forges and trip-hammers, as well as rolling and slitting mills, were in operation all through the inland region of southern New England in 1810. For the furnaces the three requisites to profitable operation were a supply of iron ore, a plentiful supply of wood to produce the char coal used as fuel, and a stream of water to furnish power for the bellows. These requisites seem to have been met best in two localities; in Litchfield County, Conn., and in a small area in south-eastern Massachusetts, including towns in Plymouth and Bristol Counties. In Litchfield there were in 1810 four furnaces, 32 forges, 8 trip-hammers, and 2 rolling and slitting mills. These works were rather evenly distributed among 16 towns, those most interested being Salisbury, Canaan and Kent.[3] In the first of these there was a famous mine from which 4,000 to 5,000 tons of ore of excellent quality were annually taken. Iron was also mined in Kent and limestone was procured in Canaan.

The principal articles produced from iron in this county were anchors and other forms of ship-hardware, bells, cart and wagon-tires, sleigh-shoes, scythes, gun-barrels, bar and sheet-iron, and nail-rods. Up to 1810 this industry seems to have had little if any appreciable effect in creating a non-agricultural population in the county.

[1] Bailey, James M. History of Danbury, Conn. New York. 1896. p. 217.

[2] Coxe, Tench. View of the United States, pp. 158–159. In this place there were 17 hatters' shops, producing 10,000 hats annually.

[3] Pease and Niles' Gazetteer gives us facts concerning the extent of the iron manufacture in these towns at a somewhat later date, 1819. There were then in Canaan 8 forges, 7 anchor shops and 2 furnaces; in Kent there were several mines in operation and 7 forges, with an estimated total output of 100 tons annually. Salisbury had 3 forges, 2 blast furnaces, 1 shop making anchors and screws, another making scythes, and 2 shops fitted with trip-hammers operated by water power which produced gun-barrels, sleigh-shoes and hoes.

The largest towns, Litchfield and New Milford, had populations of 4,600 and 3,500 respectively, but in neither of them was there any industrial development beyond the artisan activities which were regularly found in agricultural communities. Their growth was based upon exceptionally large area[1] and upon exceptional opportunities enjoyed by their inhabitants in getting produce to market. On the other hand, the towns in which the iron manufacture was most important were considerably smaller, Salisbury having 2,700 people, Canaan 2,200 and Kent 1,800.

The iron industries in south-eastern Massachusetts depended on the bog ore which was dug or dredged from the bottom of their shallow ponds.[2] Another valuable asset were the tracts of small pines and oaks, which furnished a plentiful supply of charcoal for fuel. At the beginning of the century there were 14 blast furnaces, 6 air furnaces, 20 forges and 7 rolling and slitting-mills in this region. The furnaces turned out on an average 75 to 90 tons of cast-iron each year, the forges had a capacity of about 50 tons of bar-iron and the rolling and slitting-mills produced about 200 tons each annually.[3] The furnaces gave employment to about eight or nine men each, when they were in operation. Besides nails and nail-rods, which seem to have been the staple product, these works manufactured agricultural implements, such as spades, shovels and scythes, wire teeth for wool and cotton cards, saws and edge tools, buttons, cannon-balls and firearms, anchors, bells, sheet-iron and iron utensils.

The towns of Taunton, Plymouth, Middleborough, and Bridge-water[4] were those most engaged in this industry, although a half-dozen or more neighboring towns had a furnace or a forge or two apiece. The total annual output from the works in Taunton was estimated in 1810 at 800 tons, including 350 tons of nails and 200 dozen spades and shovels.[5] In Plymouth there were rolling and

[1] Litchfield contained 72 square miles and New Milford 84.

[2] One of these ponds, in the town of Kingston, was said to have yielded 3000 tons of this ore in the space of a few years. A full description of the various sorts of bog-ore found in this region and of the methods of obtaining it will be found in the Collections of the Massachusetts Historical Society. Series I. Volume 9, pp. 254–256. Ore was also imported in small quantities from New Jersey for these works.

[3] Bishop, History of American Manufactures. I. 492. See also Mass. Hist. Soc. Coll. I. 9: 263.

[4] These were all larger in population than the typical inland town. Bridge-water, the largest town in New England off tide water, had 5150 people. The others ranged from 3900 to 4400.

[5] Morse, Gazetteer, 1810.

slitting-mills whose principal produce was nail-rods, of which they turned out about 100 tons per year.[1]   In Bridgewater scythes, axes, edge-tools, muskets and cannon were produced.   The manufacture of nails was the particular branch of this industry pursued in Middle-borough.   The ore was dredged from ponds within the town limits, smelted in local furnaces and rolled and slit into nail-rods.   These rods were later turned into nails by the farmers of the town in winter. This union of agriculture and manufactures was commented on by travelers.[2]   In fact, it seems to have been prevalent all through this section.   The business of the inhabitants of a typical town in Plymouth County was thus described in 1814: "Supplying the fur-naces with coal (*i.e.*, charcoal), and Plymouth with fuel, together with the sale of a surplus of rye, and some other productions, are the usual resources of the inhabitants, most of whom are farmers, with some mechanics; and in the summer months furnishing a few fisher-men from Plymouth."[3]   Here we see that although somewhat of a market was now open to the farmers, due to the extension of the iron industry, yet agriculture and manufacture are not yet separate industries.

Of the iron manufacture in Rhode Island Bishop says: "Manu-factures of iron, including bar and sheet-iron, steel, nail-rods, and nails, farming implements, stoves, pots, and other castings and house-hold utensils, iron-works for ship-builders, anchors and bells, formed the largest branch of productive industry in the State toward the close of the eighteenth century."[4]   In Providence County where the bulk of the manufacture was carried on, there were in 1810, 20 trip-hammers, 2 furnaces and 1 rolling and slitting-mill.   Since many of the towns in which these and other works were located were also engaged in commerce, the effect of this industry in creating a non-agricultural population can best be discussed in a later section.[5]

---

[1] Morse, Gazetteer, 1810.

[2] Dwight, Travels, II. 31 says: "In the winter season the inhabitants of Mid-dleborough are principally employed in making nails, of which they send large quantities to market. This business is a profitable addition to their husbandry; and fills up a part of the year, in which, otherwise, many of them would find little employment." See also Mass. Hist. Coll. I. 3:2.

[3] Mass. Hist. Coll., II. 4:276. Similar conditions are described in Wareham and Kingston. Ibid. II. 4:286, and II. 3:205–207.

[4] History of Manufactures, I. 503.

[5] See infra pp. 281-282.

Shoemaking.

Shoemaking was carried on by the village cobblers, either in itinerant fashion, traveling from farm to farm, or as a handicraft in their shops on the village street. Here they produced, either from their own material or from that which was brought to them by customers, goods to supply merely the demand of the local market. A wider market seems first to have been furnished in any proportions by the demand for ready-made shoes for the Continental army during the Revolution. This demand was supplied principally by certain towns in Massachusetts. As early as 1778 men's shoes for the wholesale trade were being made in Reading and in Braintree. In Lynn the transition from the handicraft to the commission stage of the industry had taken place somewhat earlier. In 1795 President Dwight found 200 master workmen employed there with 600 apprentices, carrying on their trade in little shops beside their homes along the village street. Their annual output was estimated at from 300,000 to 400,000 pairs of women's and children's shoes which they sold in Boston, Salem and other seaports.[1] Some were destined for consumption in those cities, but the larger part were shipped thence to the Southern states and the West Indies. In Connecticut shoes were made for export in Guilford, Durham, New Canaan and Woodstock.[2] In none of these towns did the population amount to 3,000 in 1810, except in Lynn and Guilford, and in both of these commercial and fishing operations were partial causes of concentration.

Woolen Cloth.

The manufacture of woolen cloth in small factories had begun as early as 1790 in southern New England, but up to 1810 the industry had had a very slow growth. In addition to the high price of labor, which hampered all attempts at manufacture at this period, there were the added difficulties of inexperience with the new spinning machinery, lately imported from England, and the unsatisfactory character of the supply of the domestic wool both in quantity and quality. The new factories were situated for the most part in small towns;[3] they employed but few hands and turned out an annual out-

[1] Dwight, Travels, I. 422.

[2] These facts have been taken from the historical sketch of the boot and shoe industry in the Census of 1900, Part III.,Vol. IX., p. 754 and from Hazard, Blanche E., Organization of the Boot and Shoe Industry in Massachusetts Before 1875. Quarterly Journal of Economics, Vol. XXVII., pp. 236–262.

[3] In Massachusetts such factories were established in Ipswich, 1792; in Newbury, 1794; in Monson, 1800; in North Andover, 1802; in Derby, Conn., 1806; and in Peacedale, R. I., in 1804.

put which would now be considered insignificant. The largest of the five woolen mills in New England from which Secretary Gallatin received reports in 1809 employed only 28 persons.[1] The output of the only woolen mill in Massachusetts enumerated in the Census of 1810 was 6,800 yards per annum, while that of two mills in Kent County, Rhode Island, was 11,000 yards for both. Altogether there were, perhaps, 20 or 25 such factories in southern New England in 1810.[2] The mills established by General Humphreys at Derby, Conn., shortly after 1800, described in Dwight's Travels, III. 375–377, are hardly typical. Besides carding and fulling machines of improved pattern they contained two jennies, a billy with 40 spindles, two newly invented shearing machines, four broad looms, eight narrow looms, and eighteen stocking frames. One writer says: "This is a fairly complete picture of the best woolen mill that existed in the United States up to the War of 1812. For its day it was far in advance of the times, and far superior to many which existed a quarter of a century later."[3]

Cotton Spinning.

Although the birth of the cotton manufacturing industry in New England, and in the United States as well, is formally dated from the arrival of Samuel Slater in Providence, Rhode Island, and the erection of the first cotton mill there in 1790, yet up to 1807 the growth had been inconsiderable, only 15 factories employing some 6,000 spindles having been put into operation.[4] A great stimulus was given to the new industry in the next few years by the prohibition of the import of foreign-made goods in the Embargo and Non-Intercourse Acts of 1807 and 1809, so that at the end of 1809 Secretary Gallatin had received reports from 62 mills in operation with a total of 31,000 spindles.[5] In the reports collected by the census officials in 1810,

[1] Gallatin's Report on Manufactures. American State Papers, Finance, Vol. II, p. 434. This mill was situated in Warwick, Rhode Island, and produced 10,000 yards annually.

[2] According to the Digest of Manufactures prepared by Tench Coxe from the Census returns of 1810, there were 15 mills in Connecticut, 2 in Rhode Island, and only 1 in Massachusetts. The returns for the last state were defective, however, and perhaps a half dozen or more mills were in operation there. See Dickinson, R., Geographical and Statistical View of Massachusetts. 1813. p. 66.

[3] North, S. N. D. The New England Wool Manufacture. In the New England States (W. T. Davis, editor). 4 vols. Boston. 1897. Vol. I., p. 205.

[4] Gallatin, Op. cit., p. 427. Twelve of these were in Rhode Island, two in Massachusetts, and one in Connecticut.

[5] Ibid.

Coxe found that there were 96 cotton manufacturing establishments in southern New England; 54 in Massachusetts, 28 in Rhode Island, and 14 in Connecticut.[1] The district of greatest concentration was then an area within a radius of 30 miles from Providence, including towns in all three states. Here there were 26 mills, with about 20,000 spindles.[2] The mills were mostly small, having on an average 600 to 800 spindles. Such a mill would employ about 40 persons, 5 men and 35 women and children.[3] Up to this time spinning was the only operation carried on in these mills, the power looms not being introduced until about 1815.[4] Meanwhile the yarn was given out to the farmers in the vicinity to be woven into cloth in their homes.

Summary

In summarizing these facts we must again emphasize the real meaning of the term "manufactures." In the only sense in which it is significant for the purposes of this essay, and, indeed, for any economic history, it includes only articles produced for a wide market, by persons who depend entirely upon the income derived from such activity for their support. Of manufactures in this sense we may say that there were practically none in New England in 1810. We found that among the many articles listed as manufactures in the official reports of the period 1790–1810, by far the greatest part were either produced in farm-houses for family consumption, such as homespun cloth, soap, candles, maple-sugar, etc.,[5] or by village artisans for local demand, as, for instance, the products of the saw-mill, the grist-mill, the tannery, or the hatter's shop. A few instances were found of articles such as paper, tinware, buttons, and other "Yankee notions," which, through an ingenious method of marketing, were disposed of over a large area. Yet their production required no organization of industry on a large scale, nor did it lead to the concentration of a non-agricultural population. Only in the case of a very few industries is a separation of employments apparent. We have seen how imperfect this separation was in the iron industry. In the shoe industry, although factory methods had not yet been introduced, still the width of the market supplied had made the

---

[1] Digest of Manufactures. There were also three factories in the District of Maine, twelve in New Hampshire, and one in Vermont.

[2] Gallatin, Op. cit., p. 433.

[3] Ibid. p. 427.

[4] Hammond, M. B., The Cotton Industry. Publications of the American Economic Association. New Series. No. 1. New York. 1897. p. 241.

[5] See also infra, Chapter VI.

workers much more independent of the soil. Finally, in the new-born woolen and cotton industries we find great, although as yet undeveloped, possibilities for the creation of a manufacturing population. None of the towns in which these industries were carried on had a population of 5,000 persons,[1] except those such as Middletown, Hartford and Providence where commercial activity was, as we shall see, the principal cause of concentration. It seems hardly an exaggeration to say that there were no inland manufacturing towns in New England at this date. We must, therefore, look further for a market for agricultural products.

[1] Bridgewater, Mass., is an exception.

CHAPTER II.

THE COAST AND RIVER TOWNS.

A glance at the map of southern New England as it was in 1810 will reveal the fact that all of the largest towns in these states were at that time to be found either on the seacoast or on the largest of the navigable rivers, the Connecticut. Has this fact any significance? Were the occupations of the bulk of the inhabitants of these towns different from those of the inland towns? Had maritime industries, such as fishing, trading, and shipbuilding developed to such an extent as to lead to a clear-cut separation of occupations? Is it possible that there was in these towns a concentrated population who furnished a market for the products of inland farmers? If so, what effect did the existence of such a market have on the agricultural population? These are the questions confronting us in this chapter.

Four Groups of Commercial Towns.

For purposes of analysis we may divide the commercial towns into four groups: (1) The towns along the north shore of Massachusetts Bay from Boston to Newburyport; (2) those on the south coast of Massachusetts, on Narragansett Bay and in Connecticut along the shore of Long Island Sound, including all the ports from New Bedford to New York; (3) the towns on Cape Cod, Martha's Vineyard and Nantucket; and (4) the river towns of the Connecticut Valley.

(1) On Massachusetts Bay.

The most important of these groups of towns was the first mentioned. Here were seven towns, not including Boston, ranging in population from 4,600 to 12,000, making a total altogether of 46,000 people. Add to this 34,000 for Boston and 5,000 for Charlestown, (at that time practically a part of the larger city) and we have a total of 85,000 persons living on a narrow strip of sea-coast some 50 miles in extent. It might well be expected that a large proportion of this population was supported by some non-agricultural activity. As far as Boston and Charlestown were concerned, there seems to have been a thorough divorce from the soil. On the little peninsula on which these cities were built there were about 3,000 houses. Their inhabitants were engaged in commerce with Europe and the West Indies, as well as with towns along the coast, and in a variety of manufactures. The importance of the commerce may be seen from the fact that for the years 1801–1810 the goods imported here had an average annual value of about $10,000,000. About 100,000 tons of shipping were owned in the city and the entries of foreign vessels alone amounted to 900 or 1,000 every year. Of the manufactures the distillation of rum seems to have been most important, 30 plants being devoted to that purpose. In 1796 rum was the principal export. Sugar was refined in eight plants, cordage made in eleven rope walks. Other manufactures were hats, plate-glass, tobacco, chocolate, sail cloth and paper. The shipbuilding business was active in Charlestown.[1]

The effect of this market for agricultural produce was evident enough to create considerable comment. Travelers were impressed with the density of population and with the evident prosperity of the farming towns nearby. Rochefoucauld says that the road from Marlborough to Boston (a distance of 27 miles) was almost a continuous village of handsome houses.[2] President Dwight says: "From Weymouth (11 miles) the country may be considered as one continual village, raised up by the commerce of Boston and forming a kind of suburb to the capital."[3] Much evidence, also, is available concerning the stimulus which was given to improved agriculture. Dickinson, writing in 1812, says: "A market for all varieties of fruit and vegetables is found in Boston. Hence the surrounding country although not especially fertile is highly cultivated."[4]

Besides the encouragement of market gardening, an increased attention to cattle-raising was evident in one nearby town;[5] a specialization in potatoes took place in another,[6] and an increase in the price of land in a third.[7] In general, however, it should be noticed that

[1] These facts come from Morse, Gazetteer, 1810; Dwight, Travels, I. 462; Kendall, Travels, II. 260; Rochefoucauld-Liancourt, Travels, I. 479; Lambert, Travels, II. 344.

[2] Rochefoucauld-Liancourt, Travels, I. 400.

[3] Travels, III. 110. Other evidence of the same nature is found in Harriott, Struggles Through Life, II. 33, 34, 36–37; Wansey, Journal, p. 48. American Husbandry (Anonymous). 2 vols. London. 1775. I. 60.

[4] Dickinson. Rodolphus. A Geographical and Statistical View of Massachusetts. Greenfield. 1813. p. 9.

[5] Abington, seventeen miles from Boston. Mass. Hist. Soc. Coll., II. 7: 115.

[6] Brookline, four miles distant. Papers of the Massachusetts Society for Promoting Agriculture. Contained in the Agricultural Repository and Journal. 10 vols. Boston. 1796–1826. Vol. II. Papers for 1807, p. 21.

[7] Hingham, twelve miles. Rochefoucauld-Liancourt, Travels, I. 482.

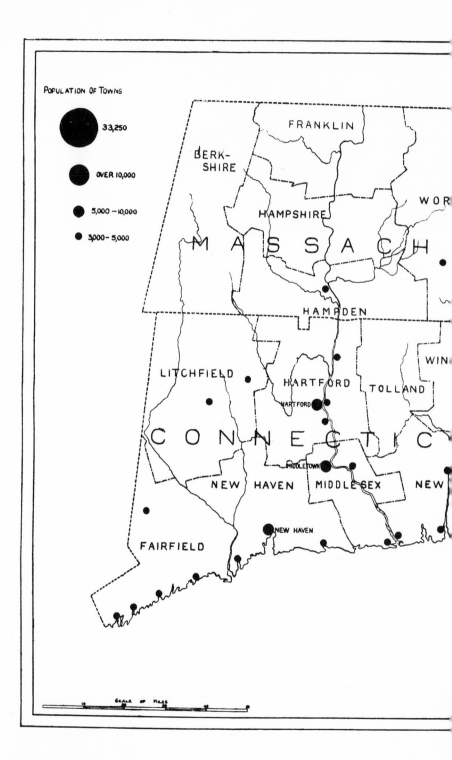

DISTRIBUTION OF POPULATION IN
SOUTHERN NEW ENGLAND
1810

this improvement was limited to a narrow area, perhaps within a 20-mile radius from the city, and at times towns well within this limit were found to be in a backward condition. For instance, a writer says of Needham: "The town in general would admit of more settlements. Much of the land is yet uncultivated; and perhaps a third more inhabitants than the present number might be supported by a more extensive cultivation of the soil."[1] And yet this town was only 13 miles distant from the city and had the advantage of water transport on the Charles River.[2] The influence of the market in concentrating population in the towns in the immediate vicinity is noticeable.[3]

In 1810, Salem was the sixth commercial city in the United States and was said to have a per capita wealth larger than that of any other city. Its population was over 12,600. Its imports averaged $3,000,000 for the years 1801–1810 and it had 40,000 tons of shipping. Besides the Asiatic trade which made this port famous, its fleet engaged in the trade to the West Indies and in the fisheries.[4] The prosperity of this city was reflected in the large population of its agricultural neighbors, the towns of Danvers and Beverly.[5]

Newburyport sustained a population of over 7,600 on exactly one square mile of land, by means of its extensive commerce and its fishing, ship-building and rum-distilling industries. It had 160 vessels in the European and West India trade and 54 more in the Banks fisheries. The latter alone carried crews aggregating nearly 500 men.[6] The rural town which benefited by this market was Newbury, a few miles farther up on the Merrimac River. It had practically no village settlement and, aside from a few fishing enterprises, its inhabitants were all engaged in farming. They culti-

[1] Mass. Hist. Soc. Coll., II. 1:180.

[2] Water transportation brought a region at a much greater distance within reach of the Boston market. This was Barnstable County which sent onions, flaxseed, corn and firewood thither. A fleet of 30 coasting vessels was said to have been regularly employed in carrying the latter product alone at this time. Mass. Hist. Coll. I. 3:14.

[3] Roxbury, 2,765; Dedham; 2,172; Dorchester, 2,930; Cambridge, 2,323. These were all towns of relatively small area.

[4] Sources for Salem are Morse, Gazetteer, 1810; Dwight, Travels, I. 408, 412. La Rochefoucauld-Liancourt estimated the fleet belonging to this port at 150 vessels, of which 100 were in foreign trade, 20 in the coasting trade, and 30 in the fisheries (ca. 1796). Travels, I. 474–475.

[5] Populations 3,127 and 4,609 respectively in 1810.

[6] These facts are from Morse, Gazetteer, 1810; Dwight, Travels, I. 400–401; Chastellux, Travels, II. 249; and Kendall, Travels, II. 29.

vated their land thoroughly and grew large crops.[1] The population of this town grew rapidly, showing an increase of 25 per cent in the decade 1800–1810.[2]

In Lynn the shoe manufacture seems to have been the chief industry of the rapidly growing population, although probably a considerable number were employed in the fisheries of Marblehead.[3] This town and Gloucester were celebrated for their fishing fleets. The former had 100 fishing vessels and 40 merchantmen, employing together in their crews some 1,100 men.[4] The Gloucester fleets employed about half that number.[5]

President Dwight sums up the fishing industry of these and other towns in Essex County as follows:

"Salem, Newburyport, Gloucester, Marblehead, Beverly, Haverhill, and Manchester are commercial and fishing towns; and contained together, in 1800, 33,620 inhabitants. (In 1810, 40,517.) To these may be added from Ipswich, Amesbury, Salisbury, Bradford, &c., enough to make the number 40,000; a greater number than are employed in this business in any county of the United States; if we except the cities of Philadelphia and New York. The commerce of this county is very great; and the fish caught and exported by its inhabitants, are more, it is believed, than one-half of all, which are exported from the Union. Its wealth is proportionally great . . . . The surface of this county is generally pleasant; the soil in most places pretty good; and the agriculture creditable to the inhabitants. The farmers are, accordingly, in good thrift."[6]

(2) *The Ports Along Long Island Sound.*

In the second general region of commercial activity, the northern shore of Long Island Sound, the principal points of concentration of

[1] The answers returned in 1807 to the questionnaire of the Massachusetts Society for Promoting Agriculture showed this town to be far in advance of others in regions farther inland. Its farmers ploughed the land destined for grain crops twice instead of once, as was usual elsewhere; and they applied fertilizers more liberally. The results were average crops which were considered high in those days. Their corn yielded 40 bushels per acre; their potatoes 200 bushels; barley, 25 bushels; rye, 20 bushels; and wheat, 10 to 18 bushels. Papers for 1807, in Vol. II., p. 15.

[2] From 4,076 to 5,176.

[3] The shoe industry we have already considered. See p. 273.

[4] Morse, Gazetteer, 1810; Dwight, Travels, I. 421; Kendall, Travels, III. 28; Rochefoucauld-Liancourt, Travels, I. 477.

[5] Morse, Gazetteer, 1810.

[6] Travels, I. 424.

the population were the cities of New Bedford, Providence, New London and New Haven. Of these Providence was by far the most important. It was not only the seat of an extensive coasting trade and port of entry for large quantities of foreign commodities, but was also the chief manufacturing town of New England. We have seen what rapid strides the cotton industry made in its vicinity, especially in the years 1807–1810.[1] President Dwight was informed that at this time five-eighths of the population of this city (10,071 in 1810), were directly or indirectly employed in this manufacture.[2] The same writer considered the woolen mills here the most extensive in the country. They were remarkable for the use of power from a 30 horse-power steam engine. The output was about 200 yards of broadcloth per diem.[3] Other industries carried on here were rum-distilling, shipbuilding, sugar-refining and the refining of whale oil. The activities of the little adjacent town of North Providence (16 square miles, 1,758 population) should be included in any description of the larger community. A fall in the Pawtucket River at this point furnished excellent water power. Dwight says: "Of this advantage the inhabitants have availed themselves. There is probably no spot in New England, of the same extent, in which the same quantity or variety of manufacturing business is carried on."[4] Among the industries which he enumerates are an iron furnace, a slitting-mill, a machine for cutting screws, three anchor forges, a cotton manufactory and three snuff-mills. The cotton manufacture had arisen also in a number of towns on the shores of Narragansett Bay near Providence. Of these Warwick and Smithfield were the most important. Both of these towns had about 3,800 inhabitants, who, besides farming, engaged in the coasting trade along the Sound.[5]

This combined manufacturing and commercial interest, centering in Providence, had a plainly noticeable effect on the density of settlement along the shores of the bay. The country immediately surrounding the city was so "lean" that it could scarcely support its own inhabitants; consequently a wider area than would be usual was affected. Attleborough and Rehoboth in Massachusetts, distant some ten to twelve miles by land, grew rapidly in population and

---

[1] Supra, pp. 274-275.
[2] Travels, IV. 477–479. Among those "indirectly interested" he includes the workmen of all sorts whose labor was necessary for the erection of factories, etc.
[3] Ibid., p. 480.
[4] Op. cit., II. 18.
[5] Morse, Gazetteer, 1810; Kendall, Travels, I. 330.

prosperity as a result.[1] Kendall says of the town of Portsmouth, on an island in the bay some 15 miles distant: "The lands on this island, which are rich and dear, are often divided into much smaller portions than is usual in the United States in general; but they are then employed in raising culinary vegetables for the consumption of Newport and more distant places. Fifty, twenty, and even ten acres, are in many instances the extent of a farm, or rather garden-ground."[2]

A calculation of the density of population in the ten towns nearest to Providence around the shores of the Bay, gives some striking figures; these towns varied from 52 to 290 persons per square mile. In only one, North Kingston, did the figure fall below the average for the state, 61.6 per square mile. The little town of Warren had a density of over 290 on its four square miles; Bristol had 224; North Providence 110; and Portsmouth 105. The average density for the ten towns was 103.2.[3] When this figure is compared with the normal density of an inland agricultural town, 45 to 50 per square mile,[4] a very marked difference is apparent. Without doubt the greater density was due to the employment of a part of the population in non-agricultural pursuits. The opportunity of supplying this body of people, and also the West India market, encouraged the farmers to more intensive cultivation and hence the supporting power of the land was increased to a point far beyond that of inland regions.

New Bedford had 5,600 inhabitants, of whom a considerable proportion lived in a village of 300 houses. They were engaged in ship-building and in the carrying trade, principally between New York and the ports of southern Europe. Some ships were also engaged in trading from this port to the East and West Indies. Its fleet consisted of 90 to 100 ships and brigs, of about 250 tons each, and 20 to 30 small vessels; their crews numbered in all from 1,000 to 1,500 men.[5] The nearby town of Westport is said to have profited by the market in New Bedford.[6]

[1] Dwight, Travels, II. 18.

[2] Travels, II. 6.

[3] These figures were obtained by dividing the Census figures for 1810 by the areas given in Pease and Niles' Gazetteer.

[4] The average density of population in six inland counties in Massachusetts was 48 per square mile; in Connecticut the figure for three inland counties was 42.

[5] Kendall, Travels, II. 215–216; Dwight, Travels, III. 58; Mass. Hist. Coll., II. 3:18. The formerly prosperous whaling business had declined ca. 1810.

[6] Dwight, Op. cit., III. 57.

Returning to the mainland, we find that between Providence and New York almost every town dabbled somewhat in commerce, sending out ten or a dozen small vessels more or less regularly to engage in carrying food supplies and firewood to the West Indies, New York and the Southern states. Some carried on small manufactures and others built a few ships each year. Stonington, Conn., furnishes a typical example. It owned 1,100 tons of shipping, including ten or fifteen fishing vessels, three regular packet-sloops running to and from New York, and one sealing ship. Perhaps a third of its 3,000 inhabitants lived in a village of 120 houses clustered about the wharves. Such a community would demand little in the way of food products which could not be supplied within its own limits.[1]

There are only three towns of this group, New Haven, New London and Norwich, all in Connecticut, which deserve especial attention. Concerning the first of these considerable detailed information is to be found in the Statistical Account of the City of New Haven by Timothy Dwight, at that time president of Yale College.[2] The principal interest of its 7,000 inhabitants was foreign and domestic commerce. This was carried on by a fleet of about 80 vessels, three-fourths of which were in the former branch. Some twenty of these were comparatively large ships, carrying crews of forty men and boys. They made extended voyages to the seal-fisheries of the Pacific Ocean, bringing back surprising profits to their owners.[3] The exports of this port averaged $560,000 a year for the years 1801–1809, and the imports $390,000 during the same period. Besides this there was some business done in the re-export of foreign commodities, amounting on the average to $56,000 a year.[4] Some manufacturing was done for export as well as for the local market. In 1806 the principal wares of this sort sent out were candles, 120,000 lbs.; leather, 20,000 lbs.; and nails, hats and shoes in smaller quantities.

Enough material is accessible to furnish a complete and detailed

---

[1] These facts are taken from Pease and Niles, Gazetteer. Other towns along the Connecticut coast, described there, had interests similar to those of this town but, in general, on a smaller scale. They were Groton, Lyme, Saybrook, Killingworth, Guilford, Stratford, Fairfield, Norwalk, Stamford, and Greenwich.

[2] Published by the Connecticut Academy of the Arts and Sciences. Vol. I., No. 1, New Haven. 1811.

[3] For a description of this business see Trowbridge, Thomas Rutherford. Ancient Maritime Interests of New Haven. In The New England States. (W. T. Davis, ed.) 4 vols. Boston. 1897. Vol. I., pp. 780–788.

[4] Dwight quotes these figures from a report of the Secretary of the Treasury. Travels, I. 158.

account of the occupations of the inhabitants of this town in 1810. The commercial interest was represented by 29 houses concerned in foreign trade, 41 dry goods stores and 42 grocery stores. There were about 300 craftsmen of all sorts, the carpenters heading the list with 50 men. The professional classes numbered 48, of whom 16 were teachers in the public schools and the same number lawyers. Adding to this total some 200 clerks, assistants and helpers, we arrive at a figure, 700, which would include all these persons and might be taken as the sum of the non-agricultural class. To estimate what proportion of the total population they and their families formed, this figure should be multiplied by 5.47, the average size of a family in the town.[1] The sum thus obtained is 3,829 persons, or less than 55 per cent of the total population,[2] who may be thought of as being supported by occupations other than agriculture. They lived in a compact settlement of 750 houses in the center of the town and carried on their businesses, trades and professions in an equal number of shops and stores.

How did the remaining 3,100 people, or 45 per cent, get their living? It is only logical to assume that they were farmers, and the testimony of travelers supports this assumption. Lambert found several large fields of maize growing in the center of the town.[3] Dwight says: "The supplies of flesh and fish are ample, and of vegetables, sufficient for the demand of the inhabitants, most of whom are furnished from their own gardens."[4] In his Statistical Account he gives a detailed list of the vegetables raised in these gardens.[5] La Rochefoucauld-Liancourt, writing some fifteen years earlier, had said: "Most of them (the inhabitants) have farms in the neighborhood, which supply provisions for their families. These small possessions in the hands of the towns-people, make it impossible for those who have a surplus of produce to find a sale for it in New Haven; it is, accordingly, sent to New York."[6] Wood, however, was an important import,

[1] This, of course, on the assumption that each person in the above enumeration was the head of a family. In case this assumption were not justified, the proportion of the non-agricultural to the total population would be even smaller. The figure 5.47 is taken from a computation made in 1787. See Statistical Account, p. 80.

[2] To this figure might be added the 60 paupers then supported from the town treasury.

[3] Travels, II. 297. His visit was made either in 1807 or 1808.

[4] Travels, I. 162.

[5] Pp. 23–24.

[6] Travels, I. 523. The importance of this trade with New York will be considered later. See infra p. 295.

about 7,500 cords being necessary each year for fuel. This was brought from neighboring coast and river towns by water. The influence of the market in New Haven, although it could not have been very great, was noticeable in the adjoining towns of Northford, North Haven and East Haven.[1]

New London and Norwich seem to have duplicated the state of affairs found in the town just described, but on a smaller scale. The first mentioned had not yet (1810) recovered from its severe treatment at the hands of Benedict Arnold during the Revolution. Its principal non-agricultural interest, fishing, employed some 55 small vessels, besides a half-dozen or more brigs which exported a large part of the yearly catch to England. Of its 3,300 inhabitants perhaps one-half lived in a compact village, which besides 300 to 400 dwellings, contained 80 to 100 stores and taverns. Considering the diminutive area of the township, four square miles, it is probable that most of its food supplies were brought across the Thames River from the large and prosperous town of Groton.[2]

Norwich, with five times the area of New London, had only a few hundred more inhabitants. Besides the usual coasting trade[3] and the building of a few ships yearly, they engaged in a variety of small manufactures, being favored by cheap transportation, via the Thames and the Sound, and exceptionally good water power. Some of the articles there produced were: iron bars and wire, buttons, clocks and watches, chocolate and earthenware. There was no considerable concentration of population in this town, its three villages having perhaps 50 to 100 houses each.[4]

(3) Connecticut River Towns.

Another region in southern New England where a population might have been supported by commerce was the valley of the Connecticut River, from Springfield to the Sound. Here an area of

[1] Dwight, Travels, I. 182; II. 40, 486.

[2] The facts concerning New London are taken from Morse, Gazetteer, 1810; Pease and Niles, Gazetteer; Kendall, Travels, I. 293–295; and Dwight, Travels, II. 502.

[3] As we shall see later, the exportable products of a considerable inland area found their outlet at Norwich. Dwight had high expectations of the future importance of this trade. He says: "At a future day it must, I think, be one of the there most commercial places in Connecticut. For a great part of the eastern division of the state, it must ever be the most convenient port; and there are now turnpike roads branching to it from almost every town in this region." Dwight, Travels, II. 33.

[4] For Norwich see Dwight, Op. cit., loc. cit.; Kendall, Travels, I. 303–304; Morse, Gazetteer, 1810; and Pease and Niles, Gazetteer.

roughly 800 square miles sustained 54,000 persons, an average of 67.5 to the square mile. But of the 16 townships into which this area was divided, only two show any considerable size. The fertility of the soil for which this valley was noted, rather than any great amount of non-agricultural activity, seems to have been the cause of a density of population not generally found at this time in farming communities. All the towns below Hartford owned a few small vessels that traded along the coast and to the West Indies. Some built a few ships and occasionally we find the beginning of manufactures, as in the case of the paper, glass, and powder mills of East Hartford,[1] and the gin-distilling business in Windsor and East Windsor.[2] The river furnished such cheap transportation that even so bulky a commodity as building-stone could be quarried in Chatham and East Haddam and marketed in Boston and New York.[3]

Hartford had in 1810, 6,000 inhabitants, of whom perhaps one-half were concentrated in a village of 400 to 500 houses in the center of the town. Here also were the shops, stores and wholesale trading houses. As Hartford was not a port of entry at the time, its commerce is hard to estimate.[4] Its trade with regions farther inland, especially the towns lying on both sides of the river for 200 or more miles to the northward, was quite large. As a depot for the transshipment of agricultural products, and especially those important by products of pioneer agriculture, potash and pearl ash, Hartford was much more favorably situated than either New Haven, Norwich or New London.[5] It is probable that a large part of the commercial wealth of the place was derived from this source. Besides the usual craftsmen, which were well represented there, Hartford seems to have had little industrial activity.[6]

[1] Dwight, Travels, II. 268.

[2] Pease and Niles, Gazetteer, pp. 65, 90.

[3] Ibid., pp. 279–280.

[4] The nearest indication I have been able to find is contained in the papers submitted with the Application for a Branch of the Bank of the United States in Hartford (1817). MSS. in library of the Connecticut Historical Society, Hartford, Conn. According to a list (E) there included, 278 vessels paid toll in Hartford in 1816. Of these 189 were sloops; 61, schooners; 26, brigs, and 2, ships. There were also 300 entries not liable to duty. These were probably the flat-boats, rafts and smaller craft from up the river.

[5] This is made clear by a map among the papers referred to in Note 4. See also Dwight, Travels, I. 203–204; and Kendall, Travels, I. 86–87.

[6] The woolen mill described by General Washington in his diary in 1788, quoted in Bishop, American Manufactures, I. 418, had been established only a short time. It ran rather irregularly and was poorly equipped. See Wansey, Journal, p. 60.

Middletown depended for its prosperity chiefly upon its commerce. Since the entries at the port included goods and ships of Wethersfield and Hartford, they give us but little clue to the trade of the city itself.[1] In 1815 there were 24 vessels, measuring altogether 3,500 tons, owned here. Up to 1810 the following manufactures had been established: A rum distillery with an annual output of 600 hogsheads; a paper mill employing 9 to 12 men; a powder mill whose product was worth $1,000 per annum; and a cotton factory, erected 1808, of 330 spindles. The inhabitants numbered 5,300 of whom a part lived in a village of 300 houses. The small influence which this settlement exerted as a market for agricultural produce may be seen in the declining population of the outlying districts. In Field's Statistical Account of Middlesex County we read: "The inhabitants of the southern, western and northern parts of this town (Middletown), are very generally farmers, and as the lands in those parts have long since been taken up for farms, the population has increased very little for many years. There were 80 dwellings in Middlefield (a village in the south-western part of the town), in 1745, and but one more in 1815. The population of Westfield, for the same length of time, has been nearly stationary. . . . Young enterprising men, trained to husbandry, unable to get farms in their native town have removed from time to time, to other parts of the country."[2] Had there been opportunity for the sale of a considerable amount of agricultural produce in Middletown, either for consumption by the merchants and artisans or for export to the West Indies, this emigration would undoubtedly have been checked.[3]

(4) Cape Cod and Nantucket.

There were two other districts in Massachusetts where maritime enterprises employed a considerable population, who purchased their food-stuffs either from the farmers in their vicinity or from those in other parts of the state. These were Barnstable and Nantucket Counties, the former including Cape Cod and the latter the island and town of the same name. Cape Cod was recognized as a unique

---

[1] Dwight, Travels, I. 190, gives a table showing the value of the imports for this district during the years 1801–1810. The annual average was $292,000. Here, as in other tables of the sort given by this author, the value of the imports is calculated from the amount of duties paid, assuming an average rate of 25%.

[2] Field, Op. cit., 38–39. The facts quoted in the description of Middletown are from this work, pp. 32–53.

[3] See Appendix B. Emigration from Inland Towns in Southern New England, 1720–1820.

region by the travelers of the period and at least two of them devote considerable space to its description.[1] They divide the Cape in general into two parts; an eastern section, from the elbow to Provincetown, and a western section, from the same point to the mainland at the town of Barnstable. The total population of the county, somewhat over 22,000 in 1810, was divided almost equally between the two sections. On the eastern end of the Cape, fishing and shipping seem to have been much more important than agriculture. All the men in the prime of life were employed at sea, leaving as a labor force to cultivate the fields only the boys and old men. Their exertions were able to draw only the scantiest of crops from the thin and sandy soil. Consequently not only beef, flour, and grain, but even fodder for the cattle, and in the winter, butter, vegetables and cheese must be imported. Some of these products came from the more largely agricultural towns to the westward, others from Boston, and the supplies of rye and maize in part even from the Southern states.[2] Yet such was the productivity of the "ocean farms" that these supplies could be purchased in sufficient quantity to support a population of considerable density,[3] in fairly good circumstances.[4]

On the sand flats at the end of the Cape, in Provincetown, there lived some 200 families who got their living entirely from the sea. Perhaps in no other town in New England could a population have been found so completely non-agricultural. The reason is obvious. There was no soil to be cultivated. "The earth," says Dwight, "is here a mere residence, and can scarcely be said to contribute at all to the sustenance of man. All his support and all his comforts, are elicited from the ocean."[5] A small meadow of marsh grass pastured two horses, ten yoke of oxen, and 140 cows, the sum total of

[1] Dwight and Kendall. The former visited Cape Cod in 1800 and described it in his Travels, Vol. III., pp. 63–97. The latter's visit, made in 1807, is described in his Travels, Vol. II., pp. 127–183. A considerable amount of information concerning the towns in this region, though of a somewhat earlier date, is to be found in the Collections of the Massachusetts Historical Association, Series I., Vols. 3, 8, and 10.

[2] Even firewood had to be imported, some of it coming from Maine. Mass. Hist. Soc. Coll., I. 8:195.

[3] A writer describing the town of Dennis says: "A tract of ground not larger than Dennis with a soil so unproductive, would in an inland situation be capable of supporting few inhabitants. But when the Census was taken in 1800, there were found on it fourteen hundred souls. A great number of these persons derive their subsistence from the sea." Mass. Hist. Soc. Coll., I. 8:133–134.

[4] Kendall makes an exception in the case of Truro. Travels, II. 16.

[5] Dwight, Travels, III. 84.

live stock owned in the town. There were one or two gardens at some distance from the village, but almost all the food supply, except fish, was brought from Boston. For this the inhabitants were enabled to pay by the sale of cod, herring, bass, mackerel, and other fish caught in the waters of the bay and on the banks of Newfoundland. The annual value of the catch of the two varieties first mentioned was over $140,000. Shipping was also an active business; many of the men being employed on coasting vessels owned in Boston and in neighboring towns. On the whole, the people were industrious and lived well; many of them were even able to put by enough money to purchase farms in the interior, where they spent their declining years.

Conditions on the western end of the Cape were considerably more favorable to agriculture. Here, as in most coast regions of New England, the inhabitants divided their energies between the sea and the land. Nearly every village owned from 5 to 20, and sometimes as many as 30 fishing and coasting vessels of from 40 to 70 tons. The towns of Falmouth and Barnstable were especially active in maritime enterprise, the former having a fleet of 50 or 60 vessels, chiefly coasters of large size employed in carrying products of the Southern states to New York and Boston.[1] Agriculture, however, was not neglected in these towns. The inhabitants cultivated their soil carefully, manured it with sea-weed, and not only reaped crops sufficient for their support, but had also a considerable surplus of onions, salt hay, flaxseed and grain for exportation to the towns on the eastern end of the Cape and to Boston.

The evaporation of salt from sea-water was a quasi-manufacture carried on in many of the towns along the Cape. In all, there were, in 1802, 136 works established for this purpose. They consisted merely of a series of shallow vats or tanks, into which the water from the ocean was pumped by the power furnished by windmills. The salt thus obtained amounted to about 100,000 bushels per annum, which at that time was worth nearly $42,000. The local fisheries furnished a ready market for this product.[2] Other works of this sort were to

[1] Mass. Hist. Soc. Coll., I. 8: 127–129.

[2] The best description of these works, utilized largely by both Dwight and Kendall, is to be found in Mass. Hist. Soc. Coll. I. 8: 135–138. Dwight entertained great hopes for the future of this industry, hoping to see it extended along the eastern coast of the United States "from St. Mary's to Machias." This hope was, of course, disappointed by the discovery and development of the mineral salt deposits in New York and other states in the following decades. Travels, III. 76–77.

be found on the islands of Martha's Vineyard and Nantucket, and in a number of coast towns in Plymouth and Bristol Counties.[1]

The township on the island of Nantucket in 1810 was entitled to rank as the fourth in Massachusetts, in wealth and in the number of its inhabitants.[2] Here on an area of about 42 square miles there lived 6,800 persons, most of them in a compact village containing some 800 houses.[3] The chief industry of the place was the whale fishery, which employed a fleet of 120 ships, manned by 1,200 sailors. On the island were 15 or 20 spermaceti works, which refined the oil thus obtained and manufactured large quantities of candles. The former of these products was exported widely to the cities of the United States and to London, Marseilles and the Levant. Owing to the sterility of the soil and to the greater profit to be obtained from whaling, agriculture received scanty attention. More than one-half the area of the island was given over to the pasturage of flocks of sheep, amounting to 7,000 in all, together with cows, oxen and horses in smaller numbers. The land under cultivation amounted to 1,350 acres, about one acre to each family on an average, yielding a small amount of maize and a few vegetables. For most of their food supply, consequently, and even for firewood, the people were dependent on the mainland. Flour and Indian corn were brought in coasters from New York, Philadelphia, and Baltimore; provisions for the whaling vessels were obtained in Boston and from the shore towns in Connecticut. The only export of an agricultural nature was wool, less than one-half the total product being consumed on the island. The importance of the market in Nantucket to the farmers of southern New England seems to have been considerably diminished by the import of grain referred to above.[4]

[1] Bishop, American Manufactures, II. 97.

[2] In population this town was surpassed only by Boston, Salem and Newburyport.

[3] The best sources of information on Nantucket at this period are the Topographical Description of Nantucket, by Walter Folger, Jun., contained in the Collections of the Massachusetts Historical Society, Series I., Vol. 3, pp. 153–155, and the Notes on Nantucket in the same collections, II. 3: 18–38. See also Dickinson, Geographical and Statistical View, p. 32; and Morse, Gazetteer, 1810. St. John de Crevecoeur gives an interesting, but not altogether reliable description of the island and of the manners and customs of its people in his Letters of an American Farmer. London. 1783. pp. 114–212.

The practice of land tenure in common, which persisted in Nantucket long after it had died out elsewhere in New England, is described by Folger, Op. cit., 154.

[4] On the neighboring island of Martha's Vineyard, in Duke's County, conditions

Summary—Relation of the Maritime Industries to Agriculture.

In concluding this survey of the peculiar economic characteristics of life in the coast and river towns, let us return to the inquiries. propounded at the beginning of this chapter. We have endeavored to answer these questions specifically in the detailed consideration of the various groups of towns. In general these answers lead us to the conclusion that the maritime industries were not, at the beginning of the nineteenth century, sharply differentiated from agriculture. As Tudor pointed out, the coast population were economically a race of amphibians.[1] They got their living both from the sea and from the land; the proportion of their income which was derived from either element depending partly on the fertility of the soil in their particular locality and partly on the advantages of their situation for fishing and trading. Where the soil was sterile and sandy, as on the eastern end of Cape Cod and on Nantucket, there we found almost the entire support of the inhabitants obtained from maritime industries; but in almost all the other towns on the coast and rivers, agriculture was still the fundamental industry, as it was inland, and fishing and trading were auxiliary occupations. As accessory sources of income for farmers, the maritime industries were comparable to the occasional small manufactures carried on in inland towns; in neither case was large scale enterprise to be found, nor the sharp separation of these employments from agriculture.

Only in a few seaport towns did we find a strictly non-agricultural population, deriving their incomes from trading and fishing and purchasing therewith the products of inland farmers. Such towns were found along the north shore of Massachusetts Bay, on Cape Cod and the island of Nantucket, along the coast of Long Island Sound, and in the valley of the Connecticut River. How important

were considerably different. Here the population was only 3,300 on 42 square miles. The land was more fertile than that of Nantucket, and although a few whale ships were sent out each year from Edgarton, the principal port, the majority of inhabitants were supported by agriculture. The export of a commercial product, the wool shorn from their large flocks of sheep, was the chief point of difference between the farm life in these towns and those on the mainland. See Morse, Gazetteer, 1810. Arts. Martha's Vineyard and Edgarton.

[1] "Most of the people near the sea coast of the latter have been sailors for a time and occasionally go on some short voyage, if they find they can earn a few more dollars than by staying at home. There are many villages, where a population of farmers would be found to be good sailors in a moment if the occasion required it." Tudor, William. Letters on the Eastern States. 2 ed. Boston. 1821. p. 118, note.

to the farmers of southern New England was the market thus supplied? That the farmers in the near vicinity, say within a radius of fifteen or twenty miles, of the largest city, Boston, benefited largely from their opportunities to sell farm produce, is a well-established fact.[1] The area affected by the markets in such smaller cities as Salem, Newburyport, Providence, and Nantucket was narrower in proportion as the numbers of their inhabitants were less. Finally in a third class of towns of 3,000 to 7,000 population, such as New Haven, New London, Norwich, Middletown and Hartford, farming seems to have been the occupation of about one-half the inhabitants,[2] and consequently the influence of their markets was hardly appreciable.

A simple calculation of the relative strength of the commercial as compared with the agricultural population may serve to make this summary more concrete:

In the nine towns on Massachusetts Bay there were....	85,000 persons
On the eastern end of Cape Cod.....................	11,000 "
In the town of Nantucket...........................	6,800 "
In five towns on Long Island Sound.................	32,000 "
In two towns on the Connecticut River..............	11,000 "
Total...	145,800

If we accept the figures for New Haven as typical of the conditions in the last two groups of towns we may subtract one-half the population of each of these groups, as representing the agricultural element in these towns. The total then becomes 124,300. This figure, it should be understood, does not represent a total of all persons in the three states of southern New England who were engaged in non-agricultural activities. It is intended merely to give an approximate indication of the size of commercial and manufacturing groups who were so concentrated as to furnish a definite and reliable market for the sale of agricultural products. These groups amounted to 15.4 per cent of the total of the three states, 809,000 in 1810; but their importance to the farmers at large was much less than this figure would indicate. A glance at the map (facing p. 277) will show how inaccessible this market was to the great body of inland farmers. Of what importance to a farmer in the center of Worcester County, Massachusetts, or in Tolland County, Connecticut, was the market in Salem, Newburyport or Nantucket? We have already seen that

[1] See supra, pp. 278–279.
[2] As we have seen in the case of New Haven, 45 per cent. were so occupied; this proportion would naturally have been larger in the smaller towns in this class.

the area affected by the largest market in southern New England extended only some fifteen or twenty miles from the city. A consideration of the transportation system of the time in a later section[1] will make even clearer that the fringe of commercial towns on the seacoast must have depended for its agricultural products upon farmers in towns adjoining, or only a few miles distant. Some exception must, of course, be made in favor of towns located on navigable rivers such as the Connecticut, the Thames, the Housatonic and the Merrimac; but in general the market in commercial towns can scarcely be said to have had any influence on the prosperity of the population or on agricultural methods in the inland region.

[1] See Chapter IV.

CHAPTER III.

COMMERICAL RELATIONS OF SOUTHERN NEW ENGLAND WITH THE SOUTHERN STATES AND THE WEST INDIES.

In our reconstruction of the economic environment of the inland farmer, we must not neglect to consider the possibility of his exporting some of the produce of his land to regions outside of New England. A market in a foreign country or in some of the other states of the Union would have been, to some extent at least, a compensation for the lack of a market in commercial and industrial towns at home, and would have modified to that extent the farmer's economic position.

Markets Outside New England: (a) New York City.

Outside New England there were three districts whose inhabitants purchased food-stuffs from the farmers in the towns of Massachusetts, Rhode Island and Connecticut. These were: (1) the city of New York; (2) the Southern states, and (3) the West India Islands. In the nearest of these markets, the city of New York, there was a population of nearly 100,000, concentrated on the island of Manhattan and a few smaller islands. This population, supported largely by commerce, offered a market larger than any in New England. It was easily accessible to the coast towns of Connecticut and Rhode Island and, to a less degree, to the towns of Berkshire County in Massachusetts and Litchfield County in Connecticut, by way of the Hudson River. However, in this case the New England farmers had to meet the competition of the energetic and progressive Dutch settlers on Long Island,[1] as well as of the nearer situated towns of eastern New Jersey and of those in New York state along the Hudson River.

We have seen that almost every town along the Sound as far east as Providence sent out small sloops to carry firewood and agricultural produce to New York.[2] In Fairfield County, the nearest county in Connecticut, the coast towns had a fleet of 20 or 30 such vessels regularly employed in transporting grain, flour, beef, pork, and potatoes

[1] See Weld, Isaac, Jun., Travels through the States of North America, . . . during the Years 1795, 1796, and 1797. 4 ed. 2 vols. London. 1807. II. 372-373.
[2] Supra, p. 283.

to the city.[1] New Haven seems to have traded with New York more extensively than any other port on the Sound. In his Statistical Account of the former city, President Dwight included a statement of this coasting trade for the year 1801, compiled from the shipping books of merchants. The largest items were: Cheese, 220,000 lbs.; pork and beef hams, 24,000 lbs.; pork, 1,900 bbls.; beef, 1,700 bbls.; butter, 800 firkins; lard, 600 firkins; corn meal, 1,000 hhds., and 1,200 bbls.; rye flour, 230 bbls.; barley, 1,500 bu.; Indian corn, 300 bu.; rye, 200 bu.; oats, 530 bu. The only vegetables shipped were beans, 280 bu.; and potatoes, 160 bu.[2]

Although these figures do not indicate any great amount of trade, yet it would be a mistake to judge the importance of the New York market by figures such as these, for the bulk of these products were not consumed in the city but trans-shipped to the West Indies.[3]

(b) Regions of Specialized Agriculture.

In order that a population supported by agriculture alone may furnish a market for the farmers in another region, it is necessary that the former shall be raising a staple product which they can sell to a wide market. To the cultivation of this staple they will then find it profitable to devote all their labor and capital. In order to secure the greatest profit from the comparative advantage which they have in the cultivation of a peculiar product, they will neglect general agriculture and rely for their food supply upon their ability to purchase from farmers in regions where such specialization has not been found profitable. Thus one of the first forms of the geographical division of labor arises.

Such a specialization was to be found in 1810 in three areas to the southward of New England. There were: (1) the tobacco plantations of the Chesapeake lowlands in Virginia and Maryland, (2) the rice and cotton plantations of the coastal plains of South Carolina and Georgia, and (3) the sugar plantations of the West India Islands.

(1) The Chesapeake Lowlands.

Cheap water transportation made these three areas almost equally accessible to the New England farmer, but their importance to him varied widely in proportion to the competition which he must face from the back-country districts of general agriculture. The size of

[1] Pease and Niles, Gazetteer, art. Fairfield.
[2] Op. cit., pp. 67–68.
[3] Kendall, Travels, I. 9.

the population engaged in specialized agriculture was also a factor of prime importance. In both these respects the area first mentioned, the Chesapeake lowlands, was of least importance. The decline of the plantation system was already evident in Virginia and Maryland in 1775. "The tobacco staple was a resource of decreasing value, and many people were finding it necessary to resort instead to the production of food-stuffs for market."[1]

A more general agriculture with considerable areas devoted to wheat and other grains, and in the back-country to cattle raising, was taking the place of the former specialization.[2] The planters in the tide-water region in 1810 were raising beef and pork, poultry and mutton, apples and other fruits in sufficient quantities for their own consumption, and wheat and corn for export.[3] The exceptional plantations which must depend on outside food supplies were very easily supplied from the back-country region where a general system of agriculture had always prevailed, for in Virginia and Maryland this region was in close contact with that of the plantations. Consequently we are not surprised to find that the New England farmers had no market in this region.[4]

---

[1] Philips, Ulrich B., Plantation and Frontier. In Documentary History of American Industrial Society. (John R. Commons, ed.) 10 vols. Vol. I., p. 83.

[2] Jefferson in his Notes on Virginia. (1787) Boston. 1832. p. 174, had noted this tendency. In his estimate of the exports are found: Wheat, 800,000 bu.; and corn, 600,000 bu., with smaller amounts of peas, beef, and pork. See also Morse, Gazetteer, 1810, art. Virginia.

As early as 1767, John Mitchell had written of this region: "The tobacco colonies enjoy a better soil and climate, [than "the more Northern colonies"] and have by that means hitherto had a good staple commodity, . . . so long as their lands are fresh and fertile; but most of them are worn out with that exhausting weed, and will no longer bear it; they are turned into Corn and Pasture grounds, which produce nothing but Corn, Cattle and Wool, as in the Northern colonies; . . . " And of Virginia in particular he says: "the soil is in general very light, and so shallow, that it is soon worn out by culture, especially with such exhausting crops as *Indian* Corn and Tobacco. It is for this reason that they are now obliged to sow Wheat, and exported fifty or sixty shiploads the last year." The Present State of Great Britain and North America. London. 1767. pp. 175–176, 177.

[3] See the description of Prince George County, Virginia, in Mass. Hist. Soc. Coll., I. 3: 89.

[4] A discussion of the commerce of Maryland is to be found in Carey, Matthew. American Pocket Atlas. 3 ed. Phila. 1805. p. 85; in Winterbotham, W. Historical, Geographical, Commercial, . . . View of the United States of America. 4 vols. New York. 1796. Vol. III., p. 43; and in Morse, Gazetteer, Art. Maryland.

(2) The Coastal Plains of South Carolina and Georgia.

On the coastal plains of South Carolina and Georgia a much different state of affairs was to be found. Here on an extremely fertile strip of lowlands, lying parallel with the coast and stretching about fifty miles into the interior, were rice swamps and cotton plantations employing large numbers of negro slaves. Through the invention of Whitney's gin in 1793, the cost of producing upland cotton had been greatly cheapened. With the increase in the demand which ensued, the production of this staple had been extended from the seacoast toward the upland region. The exports of cotton from the port of Charleston increased from 1,000,000 lbs., in 1795, to 8,300,000 in 1801. It was then of greater value than the combined exports of rice and indigo, the other two staples of this region.[1] The extension of cultivation was accompanied by an increasing specialization on the plantations. There was a tendency for the planters to neglect the production of food-stuffs and to turn their whole attention to the staple crops. This tendency is clearly observable in the descriptions of South Carolina in the period 1800 to 1810. La Rochefoucauld, writing just before the beginning of the nineteenth century, describes several plantations, of whose area a considerable proportion was then devoted to the cultivation of Indian corn, barley and potatoes. In one passage he says: "All the planters keep great numbers of oxen, cows, and pigs, which procure their food easily, and without the least expense, in the large forests which belong to the plantations."[2] The following quotation from a description of 1802, however, shows that the commercial interest had then come into the foreground. "In the husbandry of Carolina, two objects are particularly kept in view by the planters and farmers. The first is to raise something for sale; and the second is to secure provisions for family concerns. To the first the principal attention is directed; as being the source from whence all pecuniary advancements are made: while the other is only attended to, as opportunities permit. . . . In the lower country cotton and rice are cultivated largely for sale; while Indian corn, cow pease and long potatoes, are only planted sufficient for the yearly consumption of the settlement: and on many of the tide swamp rice plantations, no provisions, but potatoes, are planted; their produce being only equal to the support of the plantation for a few months. The rest is supplied by the purchase of Indian corn,

[1] Drayton, John. A View of South Carolina. Charleston. 1802. p. 118 and note.
[2] Travels, I. 598. See also pp. 586, 597.

brought down the rivers from the middle parts of the state; and also imported from some of these United States. "[1]

Lambert, writing a few years later, said in describing plantation life in this state: "Everything is made subservient to the cultivation of cotton and rice. . . . With hundreds of slaves about them, and cattle of various kinds, they are often without butter, cheese and even milk, for many weeks."[2] In 1809 Ramsay, the historian, in speaking of the increase in the cultivation of cotton and rice since 1795, said: "These two staples have so monopolized the agricultural force of the state that for several years past other articles of export and even provisions have been greatly neglected. In their great eagerness to get money the planters have brought themselves into a state of dependence on their neighbors for many of the necessaries of life, formerly raised at home."[3]

The plantation system, however, had not been extended over a very large part of the lowland region in 1810. There were still many small planters and farmers who, while devoting most of their attention to the staple products, raised sufficient grain and meat for their own consumption and that of the few negroes whom they employed. It becomes important, therefore, to delimit as closely as possible the area of large scale, specialized agriculture; for only in this way can the extent of the market for food-stuffs be determined. This may be best accomplished by an examination of the relative numbers of blacks and whites in the seacoast counties of South Carolina and Georgia. The plantation system in its full development meant the presence of large numbers of slaves with relatively few white masters and overseers. Such a system, therefore, could hardly be the rule in districts where the whites were equal or numerically superior to the blacks. Yet such was the case in all but four districts in South Carolina, and in all but five in Georgia.[4] These nine districts formed

---

[1] Drayton, View, p. 113.

[2] Lambert, Travels, II. 148. Lambert's travels were made in 1806–1808.

[3] Ramsay, David. History of South Carolina. 3 vols. Charleston. 1809. II. 214.

[4] In South Carolina:

Districts	Total Inhabitants	Slaves
Charleston	57,480	41,945
Colleton	24,903	20,471
Beaufort	20,428	16,031
Georgetown	22,938	16,568
	125,749	95,015

a continuous belt along the coast of the two states for some 250 miles. They contained in 1810 a total population of about 150,000, of whom over 110,000 were slaves. This, then, was the extent of the market for food supplies in that general region known as the Southern states.

The back-country region of these two states could have very easily supplied this market, except for the presence of a strip of pine barrens intervening between the upper country, where general agriculture was carried on, and the plantation district. This middle country, a sterile area varying from fifty to seventy miles in width, producing little in the way of food-stuffs except in the river valleys, formed a barrier to trade between the regions on either side. It was the presence of the barrier region that forced the planters of the lowlands to buy a part at least of their grain, vegetables, dairy products and salt-meat from the Middle and New England states. It would be a mistake, however, to suppose that the back-country furnished no supplies at all to the planters. The intervening region was crossed in at least three places by rivers navigable to the edge of the upper country, by vessels of 70 tons burden.[1] There was, besides, some carriage of country produce by wagons from the upper country to the coast.[2]

The products of the Middle and Northern states were carried hither in the small coasting vessels which, as we have seen, were owned in so many New England ports. They brought grain from New York and Pennsylvania; and from New England, cheese and butter, dried fish, salted beef, apples, potatoes, hay and cider. Some of the cargoes contained various products of household industry such as the coarse linen tow-cloth used for garments for the slaves,

In Georgia:

Districts	Total Inhabitants	Slaves
Chatham.	12,946	9,049
Bryan.	2,836	2,306
Liberty.	5,313	3,940
McIntosh.	2,660	1,819
Glynn.	1,874	1,092
Camden.	1,681	735
	27,310	18,941
Total for both states.	153,059	113,956

These figures are taken from the second U. S. Census (1800).

[1] See Drayton, View. pp. 30–31.

[2] Ibid. p. 141, and La Rochefoucauld-Liancourt, Travels, I. 630.

straw hats, woodenware and, finally shoes which, as we have found, had risen to the dignity of a manufacture.[1]

In this analysis we have seen the market included under that vague term "the Southern states," shrinking in reality to the population of a modern city of fair size, but spread over 250 miles of seacoast, and distant over 800 miles from the ports of New England. And besides, New England shared the privilege of feeding these 40,000 planters and their 110,000 slaves with the back-country and the Middle states. Only a few New England farmers, those in the seacoast towns and in the towns behind such ports as New Haven and New London, in Connecticut, could have had any access to this market. The mere fact that some products were shipped from such towns to a market so small and at such a distance is the best sort of evidence of the lack of any market at all at home. It shows how strenuously the farmers were trying to supply this lack and to break through the bounds of their self-sufficient economy.

(3) The West Indies.

The third region outside of New England, in which its farmers found a market for agricultural products, was the sugar-producing islands of the West Indies. There were several circumstances which made the demand for outside food supplies greater in these islands than in the cotton plantations of South Carolina and Georgia. In the first place, the raising of sugar on large plantations with slave labor had long been established and had made great progress through the eighteenth century.[2] Large importations of negroes from Africa followed, and a considerable increase in the white population. In 1810 there were probably about 2,000,000 persons in all the islands of the archipelago, of whom only a few hundred thousand were whites.[3] The principal sugar producing islands were owned by England and

[1] See Belknap, History of New Hampshire, III. 218; Gallatin, Report on Manufactures, p. 439; Bond, Phineas. Letters (1787–1794). In Annual Report, American Historical Association, 1896–1897. P. 651.

[2] The value of the exports of the English islands to the home country had increased from £629,533 in 1699 to £6,390,658 in 1798. Between the years 1699 and 1775 the amount of sugar exported to England from these islands increased from 427,573 cwt. to 2,002,224 cwt. See Edwards, Bryan. History . . . of the British Colonies in the West Indies. 3 ed. London. 1801. II. 595–598.

[3] The figures, based largely on estimates, in Morse's Gazetteer for 1817, Vol. II., app., are 2,430,000. In Worcester, J. E. Universal Gazetteer, 2 ed. Boston. 1823. Vol. II., p. 944, the sum of the population of the islands owned by various nations is put at 1,700,000.

France. Their possessions contained at this time about 1,000,000 negroes and less than 200,000 whites.[1]

We have seen that one of the reasons why the rice and cotton plantations of the South Carolina-Georgia coastal plain furnished a better market for the agricultural products of New England than did the Chesapeake lowlands was that the distance separating the plantations from the backcountry was greater in the former case than in the latter. In a certain sense it might be said that in the West India islands there was no back-country. That is, there was no sharply defined region where the commercial products could not be raised; no uplands occupied by farmers carrying on a general agriculture and selling food supplies to the planters.[2] But this is far from saying that the whole of the arable area was given over to the cultivation of the staples. The statistics given for Jamaica in 1791 show that of the 1,740,000 acres in that island under cultivation, only 767,000 were in sugar plantations, whereas an almost equal area, 700,000 acres, was used for breeding and grazing farms and 350,000 acres for raising the minor staples and provisions.[3] In Hispaniola, now called Haiti, there were in 1790, 793 sugar plantations, 789 of cotton, 3,117 of coffee, 3,160 of indigo and 623 smaller farms where yams, grain and other provisions were grown.[4] More significant, however, for we must remember that the farms were much smaller in acreage than the plantations, is the fact that even on the latter, a considerable area was given over to the pasturing of cattle and horses.[5]

Between the years 1790–1810 there had undoubtedly been much progress in the direction of specialization, especially in Jamaica.[6] Edwards had written at the former date: "In most other states and kingdoms, the first object of agriculture is to raise food for the support of the inhabitants; but many of the rich productions of the West

---

[1] Perhaps the most reliable figures for the English islands are those for 1791 given by Edwards, History, II. 2; Whites, 65,305; blacks, 455,684. For the French islands a summary of various censuses, 1776–1786, quoted by Morse, Gazetteer, 1810, gives a total of 63,682 whites and 437,736 blacks.

[2] There were highlands in the interior of many of the islands but these were so heavily wooded as to be inaccessible. See Edwards, History, I. 248–249.

[3] Ibid. I. 248.

[4] Ibid., III. 142–143.

[5] Edwards estimates that on a plantation of 900 acres, two-thirds of the land would be pasturage and woodland. Op. cit., I. 248.

[6] The negro insurrection in Haiti, 1791–1801, checked the progress of the industry in a large part of that island.

Indies yield a profit so much beyond what can be obtained from grain that in several of the sugar islands, it is true economy in the planter, rather to buy provisions from others, than to raise them by his own labor. The produce of a single acre of his cane fields, will purchase more Indian corn than can be raised on five times that extent of land, and pay besides the freight from other countries. Thus not only their household furniture, their implements of husbandry, their clothing, but even a great part of their daily sustenance, are regularly sent them from America or Europe."[1] The increase in the output of the staples and the growth of population are both evidences of this tendency to a more and more commercialized agriculture.[2]

By 1810 a large part of the timber products and food-stuffs consumed in the British islands was imported from the United States.[3] In the years 1801–1803 the average annual amounts of the principal commodities imported were: Corn, 500,000 bu.; bread and flour, 233,000 bbls.; Indian meal, 28,000 bbls.; beef and pork, 36,000 bbls.; fish (dried) 50,000 quintals; fish (fresh) 23,000 bbls. Of timber and timber products, there were annually imported from the United States: pine boards, 27,000,000 feet; 36,000,000 shingles; 12,000,000 staves; and 10,000 tons of miscellaneous timber.[4] The value of these commodities and others, such as live stock, horses, mules, dairy products and vegetables shipped from ports of the United States to the possessions of France, England, Spain, Denmark and Sweden in these islands in the ten years, 1802–1811, amounted on the average to $1,225,000 per year. In the first years of this period the annual export was considerably greater than the average, because of the

[1] Edwards, History, II. 459.

[2] Jedidiah, Morse, in The American Universal Geography. 6 ed. Boston. 1812. Vol. I., p. 666, estimates the increase in population in Jamaica at 100,000 in the period 1787–1811.

[3] The importance which the West India colonists ascribed to this trade may be appreciated by reading some of the pamphlets of a political nature printed in London 1800–1810. In the discussion of the impending war and of the advantages to be gained by opening more widely the ports of the islands to the American trade, the dependence of the West Indies on the United States for food supplies is strongly emphasized. Three typical pamphlets of this sort are Brown, Alexander Campbell. Colony Commerce. London. (ca. 1790); Jordan, G. W., Claims of the British West India Colonists. London. 1804; and Medford, Macall. Oil without Vinegar, . . . or British, American, and West Indian Interests Considered. London. 1807.

[4] These figures are obtained by division of the totals for the three years given by Medford, Oil without Vinegar, app. No. 2. He claims to have had them from official documents.

relaxation of many of the restrictions on the commerce of their colonies during the wars in which France and England were engaged. In the years 1807–1809, on the other hand, the figures fell much below the average, owing to the Embargo and Non-Intercourse laws then in effect. The figures for 1810, a normal year, were $1,229,308, corresponding quite closely with the average for the whole period.[1]

The pertinent question for the purposes of our essay is: What part of this sum represented the food products shipped from New England farms? In answering the question we must not be misled by the frequent references to the active trade carried on by the coast towns of Connecticut and Rhode Island with the West India islands. When we remember how small were the vessels employed (according to the terms of Jay's treaty of 1794 they were limited to 70 tons),[2] and that they regularly made only two voyages each year,[3] we are more likely to proceed with caution. Then there is to be considered the share in this trade which was carried from the ports of the Middle and Southern states, such as Philadelphia and Charleston. The superiority of the back-country of New York, Pennsylvania, Maryland and Virginia in the production of grain, especially of wheat, had been apparent as early as 1790.[4] In fact, the seacoast towns of the New England states were continually importing flour and grain from the Middle and Southern states, partly for consumption and partly for re-export.[5] On the other hand in the export of provisions, the three states of southern New England were at this time superior to any other group. They were credited with about one-half of the total

---

[1] These figures are taken from Seybert, Adam. Statistical Annals. Philadelphia. 1818. pp. 134 ff.

[2] Hildreth, Richard. History of the United States, rev. ed. 6 vols. New York. 1877–1880. Vol. IV. 540.

[3] This is the statement made by Jordan, G. W. Claims of Colonists. 90–91.

[4] The figures for the export of the principal grains, 1791–1792, given in Coxe, View, p. 414, are:

	Wheat	*Corn*	*Rye*
Virginia	395,000 bu.	685,000 bu.	—
Pennsylvania	131,000	414,000	10,00 bu.
New York	186,000	227,000	956
Maryland	140,000	232,000	42
Massachusetts	154	78,000	1,600
Connecticut	—	36,000	—
Rhode Island	438	5,100	—

[5] Governor Sullivan, of Massachusetts, wrote to President Jefferson in 1808: "The seaport towns are supported almost entirely by bread from the Southern and Middle States." Quoted in Adams, Henry. History of the United States. 1801–1817. 10 vols. New York. 1889–1891. Vol. IV., pp. 254–255.

exports of salted beef and pork, butter, cheese and lard, potatoes and onions; one-seventh of the hams and bacon and practically all of the fresh meat and live stock. For these products the West India islands formed the only foreign market. Assuming that the share of the New England states in this market remained constant in the next twenty years, we may form a rough estimate of the total amounts of their exports thither in 1810, by applying the proportions given above to the average annual exports of these products from the whole United States for the ten years, 1801–1810.[1] According to this calculation, the three states under consideration would have been shipping about 960 tons of butter, 486 tons of cheese, 850 tons of lard, $9\frac{1}{2}$ tons of hams and bacon; of beef and pork together, 75,000 bbls., 22,160 head of live stock and 4,000 dozen of poultry.

Estimate of the Importance of these Markets.

For a comparison of the importance of each of the three markets, in the commercial towns, in the Southern states, and in the West Indies to the New England farmer we must rely on three criteria: (1) the size of the non-agricultural or specialized agricultural population in each region, (2) the extent of their dependence on outside sources of food supply, and (3) the amount of competition from other food-producing regions for the various markets. Tested in all these ways, the West Indian market seems to have been most important. The population to be supplied was from eight to ten times as large as in either of the other two regions; it was nearly as dependent on outside supplies of foodstuffs as were the commercial towns along the coast of New England, and more so than the rice and cotton plantations in South Carolina and Georgia; and, most important of all, it had no back-country of general agriculture. This last fact, however, does not mean that the New Englanders had a monopoly of

---

[1] The average annual exports from the United States, 1801–1810, were as follows: Beef, 76,300 bbls;. pork, 59,000 bbls.; butter, 1,926,000 lbs.; cheese, 972,000 lbs.; lard, 1,700,000 lbs.; hams and bacon, 1,340,000 lbs.; potatoes, 70,000 bu.; cattle, 6,400 head; horses, 4,300; sheep, 7,760; hogs, 3,500; poultry, 4,000 dozen. All of these items, except the live stock show a considerable increase over the figures for 1791. This is especially noticeable in the figures for butter, cheese and lard, the totals for the three being over 200 per cent greater at the later date. The total of live stock had, on the other hand, decreased from 38,000 head (average for the years 1791–1794) to 22,000. This would seem to show that the farmers of New England were finding it more profitable to fatten and slaughter their stock at home and to give greater attention to dairy products as exports.

These figures are taken from Pitkin, Timothy. A Statistical View of the Commerce of the United States of America. Hartford. 1816. pp. 89–129.

the market, for in supplying this as well as the market in the Southern states they had to meet the competition of the Middle states.

The importance to the inland towns of these markets, in the Southern states, and in the West Indies, as well as in the coast towns of southern New England, depended chiefly on two circumstances: (1) upon the size of the markets, *i.e.*, the quantity of produce which they would absorb, and (2) upon their accessibility. The determining factor in the latter case was, of course, the cost of transportation. We have seen that the total amount of agricultural produce demanded by these various regions was not large. In order to estimate accurately what these markets meant to the inland farmers, we must go a step farther and determine, if possible, how the trade in farm products was distributed through the inland country. If equally distributed among the inland towns, this trade would have meant very little to any one of them; if carried on by the towns in only a few favored regions, it might have altered their economic situation considerably, but for the inland towns as a whole it would have had little significance.

In order to answer these questions fully, it is necessary to investigate the general conditions of internal trade in southern New England and especially the state of the transportation system. These matters will be taken up in the following chapter.

CHAPTER IV.

INTERNAL TRADE AND THE TRANSPORTATION SYSTEM.

In the absence of a non-agricultural population centered in manu-facturing towns and cities, the internal trade of a country must perforce be limited to the exchange of goods between the agricultural regions in the back-country and the commercial towns, if there be any, on the seacoast or on navigable rivers. The inland farmers will endeavor to secure in this way as great a quantity as possible of the commodities which they either could not produce at all, or only at too great an expense. The amount of this trade will depend chiefly on the demand for the farmers' products from the outside, upon the amount which will be taken at a price high enough to pay the costs of production and of transportation. A second determining condition is the state of the transportation system. This, however, is of only secondary importance; for with the most perfect and the cheapest means of transportation, there will be no trade unless there is somewhere a population desirous and capable of making purchases. On the other hand, if there is a steady demand for goods, strenuous efforts will soon be made to improve and cheapen the carrying system. Such improvements, of course, come tardily; it may be from lack of capital available for investment or from a failure to realize the bene-fits of such improvements; and there is always the limitation imposed by the state of mechanical and technical progress, as, for instance, in the centuries before the invention of the locomotive. Once established, it is true, a cheaper method of transportation promotes an extension of the geographical division of labor, and so stimulates and increases trade. But nevertheless, it is the market which is of primary importance as regards internal trade; for unless there is a purchasing population, either actual or potential, at one end of a route, expensive improvements of that route will never be attempted.

One of the best indications of the volume of internal trade of this sort is the size of the commercial towns. In the sea and river ports there will be a non-agricultural population of merchants and ship-owners roughly proportional to the amount of trade carried on by them between the back-country and foreign parts. Boston was the only port of New England of any considerable size at the end of the eighteenth century. Concerning this port an observing traveler had remarked that its growth was much slower than that of other eastern seaports, and had attributed this circumstance to the fact that its trade with the "back settlements" was less than that of such cities as Baltimore, New York and Philadelphia.[1] A considerable portion of the inhabitants of Boston as well as of other ports, such as Salem, Providence, New Haven and New London, were engaged in occupations quite independent of commerce with the back-country. They caught fish and exported them, and were engaged in carrying the products of the Southern states to foreign countries.

The Waterways.

We naturally look first for indications of internal trade to the waterways, which have always furnished the cheapest method of transportation. There were three large rivers running in roughly parallel courses from north to south, which furnished a means of communication between the inland towns of New England and its seaports. Near the western boundaries of Vermont, Massachusetts and Connecticut, flowed the Hudson. The few towns nearest this river in the two latter states sent small quantities of beef, cheese and grain to New York, to be consumed there or trans-shipped to the West Indies. From southern Vermont, potash and other timber products, maple sugar, furs, bar-iron and nails, live cattle and horses, and some dairy produce and provisions came overland to Troy in New York state and thence were carried down the river.[2] The towns of Albany and Hudson also served as collectors of these products and distrib-

---

[1] See Weld, Travels, I. 55. The following table shows the growth of population in these four cities 1790–1810:

	1790	1800	1810	Increase per cent
Boston.....................	18,000	25,000	33,000	94.7
Philadelphia.................	28,500	41,200	53,700	88.4
New York...................	33,000	60,400	94,000	184.8
Baltimore..................	13,500	26,500	35,600	163.7

Boston had, it is true, increased somewhat faster than Philadelphia in the period 1800–1810. This was probably due to the larger share which the former port had in the carrying trade in the years preceding the Embargo and the Non-Intercourse Acts.

[2] Lambert enumerates oak and pine staves, lumber, maple sugar, wheat, flour, butter and cheese, salt beef and pork, pot- and pearl ashes, horses and oxen as the commodities shipped from this region. Travels, II. 502–503; Mass. Hist. Soc. Coll., II. 9: 138.

utors of the West India commodities and European manufactures received in return.[1]

The principal inland waterway in eastern New England was the Merrimac River. Originally it had been navigable only as far as Haverhill, about twenty miles. Above this point its rocky bed and frequent falls had rendered it of little use in transportation of any commodities except lumber. In 1803, however, a canal was opened from Boston harbor across Middlesex County to the junction of the Concord and Merrimac rivers where the city of Lowell is now situated. Although this work represented a considerable investment of capital, its usefulness was limited by its many locks and shallow bed.[2] The principal commodities transported to Boston by this means seem to have been timber and logs. By land Boston received cattle driven in from the surrounding country and from southern New Hampshire to be slaughtered and packed for exportation, and in the winter some grain and dairy products came overland on the snow.[3]

The Connecticut River furnished the only means of cheap transportation through the central region of New England. Although originally navigable only as far as the falls at Enfield, Connecticut, some sixty-five miles above its mouth, a series of canals con-

---

[1] See Weld, Travels, I. 57. A considerable portion of this trade was diverted in the opposite direction by the restrictions of 1807–1808. It was evidently comparatively easy to smuggle goods across the frontier into Canada, and there was almost continuous water transportation via Lake Champlain and the St. Lawrence River to Montreal and Quebec, whence the goods were trans-shipped to the West Indies, their original destination. For a description of this traffic see Lambert, Travels, I. 100–104, 139–140, 225–226, 245, 250–253, 260–262; and Kendall, Travels, III. 277, 283, 294; also Williams, Samuel. The Natural and Civil History of Vermont. 2 ed. 2 vols. Burlington (Vermont). 1809. II. 365–367. This writer remarks: "The trade itself has been of great advantage, in promoting the settlement of the country; but the carriage of the articles, being chiefly by land, and through long and bad roads, has been attended with great expense; and has much prevented the raising of wheat, and other kinds of grain. Ibid. p. 366.

[2] The work when completed in 1808 cost about $500,000. It was 28 miles long and contained 22 locks. Its depth, $3\frac{1}{2}$ feet, permitted navigation by boats of 24 tons. See Gallatin, A. Report of the Secretary of the Treasury on the Subject of Public Roads and Canals. Washington. 1808. p. 51. The traffic through this canal in 1806 amounted to 9,400 tons. Morse, Gazetteer, 1810. art. Middlesex Canal.

[3] See Belknap. History of New Hampshire, III. 80–81. Rochefoucauld-Liancourt, Travels, II. 160.

structed in the years 1790–1810[1] had made possible the passage of small boats to the village of Barnet in northern Vermont, about 180 miles farther.[2] The only vessels which could be used above Hartford were flat-bottomed craft of 10 or 20 tons burden. These floated downstream easily enough, but when going in the reverse direction had to be slowly and arduously propelled by poling, with only occasional aid from small square sails when the wind was favorable. According to Dwight[3] there was at about this time a fleet of fourteen of these boats which made regular trips between Hartford and the head of navigation in Vermont. Each round trip required twenty-five days and only nine could be made in a season. Potash and pearlash, staves, shingles, grain, beef, flaxseed and linseed oil were brought down to Hartford, and rum, salt, molasses and some drygoods, iron and tea were carried back. Heavy timber was floated down in rafts.[4] The total amount of this traffic in a

[1] These canals were built around falls or rapids at South Hadley and Miller's Falls in Massachusetts; at Water Quechee, now called Sumner's Falls, in Vermont; and at falls in the town of Lebanon, New Hampshire, about three miles above White River Junction.

The canal at South Hadley was begun in 1790 and finished in 1795. It was two miles long, twenty feet wide, but only three feet deep. Originally the difference in level between the ends of the canal was overcome by means of an inclined plane. The boats were drawn on a cradle up this plane by means of a windlass operated by water power. Later, in 1805, a system of seven locks was substituted and the bed of the canal was deepened. The best description of these works is to be found in Holland, J. G. History of Western Massachusetts. 2 vols. Springfield. 1855. I. 305–307. See also Rochefoucauld-Liancourt, Travels, II. 210, and Dickinson, Geographical and Statistical View, p. 30.

The Miller's Falls canal in the town of Montague was completed in 1800. It was almost three miles long, twenty feet wide, and contained ten locks. The water from the river was diverted by means of a dam 17 feet high and 325 yards long. See Hayward, John. Gazetteer of Massachusetts. Revised ed. Boston. 1849. pp. 421–422; Dwight, Travels, II. 335.

At Bellows Falls a canal about one mile long was cut through solid rock at a cost of $90,000. See Biglow, Timothy. Journal of a Tour to Niagara. Boston. 1876. p. 118. Biglow visited the place in 1805. See also Dwight, Travels, II. 83–85.

The two other canals were smaller works and were hardly in operation before 1810. They, as well as the others, are described in Bacon, Edwin M. The Connecticut River. New York. 1906. pp. 310–324.

[2] Dickinson, Geographical and Statistical View, p. 26.

[3] Travels, IV. 142–143.

[4] This list is from Kendall, Travels, III. 218. These are the commodities most frequently mentioned in the advertisements of traders in the newspapers published in such river towns as Springfield, Northampton, Greenfield, Walpole and Hanover.

season was probably smaller than a fair-sized river steamer would now carry in a few days.[1]

At Hartford the goods received from the upper river were trans-shipped into small schooners and sloops and, together with more provisions and small quantities of vegetables, were sent down the river to New York and to the West Indies. These additional commodities seem to have been produced almost entirely by the farmers in a few towns in the immediate vicinity of Hartford and Middletown, such as Farmington[2] and Wethersfield. The towns lower down the river had practically no share in this trade[3] except in furnishing cargoes of wood for fuel. In 1789 the traffic on the lower river had employed a fleet of about 100 vessels, of which 60 made voyages to the West Indies and the remainder engaged merely in the coasting trade.[4] The foreign branch of this trade was considerably damaged by the restrictions of 1807–1808 and later by the War of 1812. In 1815 the whole value of the exports from the Middletown customs district, which included all river ports, amounted to less than $100,000.[5]

The commodities brought up the river to Hartford were the same as those carried on farther up the river, with the addition of a variety of European dress goods and some other imported manufactures, such as crockery, glassware, etc.[6]

[1] Some indication of the amount of this traffic may be gained from the figures given by Dwight, Travels, I. 287, for the tonnage locked through the canal at South Hadley, which amounted on an average to about 7,000 tons per season. At the canal at Bellows Falls 4,300 tons paid tolls in 1803 and 5,460 tons in 1807. Kendall, Travels, III. 217.

[2] See Porter, Historical Discourse, p. 46.

[3] Field says of the towns in Middlesex County that whereas they send "immense quantities" of wood to New York and other towns, they export very little beef, pork, grain and provisions, "the supply hardly sufficing for the consumption of the inhabitants." Statistical Account of Middlesex, pp. 12, 14, 17.

[4] Field, Statistical Account, p. 8.

[5] Ibid. p. 127.

[6] The general store in this region shows a far greater assortment of goods than those in inland towns, but the staple commodities on which greatest emphasis was laid were in all cases the same: Salt, sugar, molasses, rum and iron. A typical advertisement is that of Bolles, Savage and Co., appearing in the Middletown Gazette, Nov. 3, 1803. This firm has to sell 40 hogsheads of Muscavado sugar, also a quantity of molasses and of Windward Islands rum. They have "constantly on hand" iron, salt and other groceries for which they will receive all kinds of country produce in payment. Some of the commodities which they offer to buy are flaxseed, oats, corn, potatoes, rye-flour, and horses. There were in this issue advertisements of 16 such general stores besides specialized dealers

The Roads and Highways.

The Connecticut River and the two other water routes parallel with it served the transportation needs of the towns on their banks, and carried produce for farmers living within a distance of fifteen to twenty miles on either side. In the intervening territory between the three river valleys, all transportation had to proceed overland on the common highways. All roads in the country at this time were poor; those in New England only somewhat less so than in other sections. The task of laying out and repairing highways had been originally entrusted to the town governments. The selectmen of the town determined what roads were necessary and two "surveyors" were annually appointed to clear new roads and to make such repairs as they deemed advisable. No taxes were collected for this purpose, but the surveyors were empowered to call out all the able-bodied men with their teams on certain days "having respect to the season of the year and the weather" to work on the roads.[1] In spite of the fines which were imposed for neglecting this duty, many absented themselves and often those who did appear seem to have regarded the occasion as a sort of junketing party.[2]

in salt, iron and tinplate, linseed oil, paints and varnishes, leather, bottles and paper.

In another issue, that of August 5th of the same year, a general store offers to buy brown tow cloth, 10 firkins of butter, 200 bushels of potatoes, 500 ropes of onions, and 10 three-year-old mules. Other dealers will buy cider, livestock, apples, hay, rags, hides, skins, oak and hemlock bark, and beeswax.

In the columns of the Hartford Courant the same sort of advertisements appeared including, however, a somewhat greater variety of "European goods."

[1] See Province of the Massachusetts Bay, Acts and Resolves, 1693–1694. Ch. 6, Vol. I., p. 136. Also Public Records of the Colony of Connecticut, 1643. Vol. I., p. 91.

[2] In many Massachusetts towns this practice of "working out the highway tax" persisted until after the Civil War. In the Report of the (U. S.) Commissioner of Agriculture for 1866 the methods pursued and the results accomplished are described as follows: "No one who has once witnessed the process of 'mending roads' in a small New England country town, needs any argument to convince him that a system more ingeniously devised to accomplish nothing was ever invented. The surveyors, in the first place, are usually elected at the town meetings, and, as the office of surveyor is of no pecuniary profit beyond mere day wages, persons of peculiar skill, could such be found, would not usually accept it. In fact, the farmers of the district take their turns in the office, any respectable man being deemed fully competent. Often some citizen who lives on a road out of repair seeks the office, and is elected, and takes the opportunity to expend most of the tax for the year on his own road, and leaves the rest of the district to be attended to in the future. The surveyor selects, not the season when repairs

As a result, the work, if we can call it work, was most inefficiently done. It was not until about 1775 that this system began to be abolished in Connecticut and provision was made for laying taxes in certain towns for the repair of their roads.[1]

How the Roads Were Laid Out.

The roads first laid out were those serving the inhabitants of the town in passing from farm to farm and in going to and from the center of the town where stood the meeting house and country store.

are most needed, but that which is most convenient for himself and his brother farmers, after their spring work is done, or after harvesting, and notifies every person assessed to come and work out his tax. As the citizens in town meeting fix the price to be allowed for the labor of men and animals in thus working out the taxes, it is usually fixed at the highest prices which the best men and teams could command, and often much higher, every voter who intends to 'work out his tax' having a direct interest to fix a high price, and they constitute a large majority in town meeting. The time appointed 'for working out the highway tax,' as it is rightly termed, arrives, and at eight o'clock a.m. a motley assemblage gathers, of decrepit old men, each with a garden hoe on his shoulder; of pale, thin mechanics from their shoe shops, armed with worn-out shovels; half-grown boys, sent by their mothers, who, perhaps, are widows; with perhaps the doctor, the lawyer, and even the minister, all of whom understand that 'working on the road' does not mean hard labor, even for soft hands. The farmers bring their steers, great and small, with the old mare in the lead, with a cart; and the Irishman drives up with his rickety horse-cart and the mortal remains of a worn-out railroad horse, to do his part. The only effective force on the ground consists of two or three yokes of oxen and a half-dozen men hired by the surveyor with money paid by non-residents, or men whose time is of too much value to themselves to be wasted on the road. Here is the surveyor, who never held the office before, and who knows nothing of road-making or of directing a gang of hands. The work must go on in some way. The roads are soft and full of ruts, or rough with protruding stones. The stones must be covered, and the road rounded up into shape. The cattle are all put to the big town plough, which is set in at the side of the road; the boys ride on the beam, and the drivers put on the lash, and the gutters, half filled with the sand and soil and leaves of a dozen seasons, are ploughed up, the shovel and hoe men waiting very patiently for their turn to work. The teams then stand idle; and this mixture, more fit for the compost heap than anything else, is thrown upon the road, and finally leveled and smoothed by the old men with their hoes; and thus the road is mended. This is not an exaggerated picture of 'working on the road' in many small towns. The occasion is regarded rather as a frolic than as serious labor; the old men tell stories to an audience always ready to lean on their tools and listen. The youngsters amuse themselves by all sorts of practical jokes, among which is the favorite one of overloading the carts, when any carts are used, so as to stick the teams."

[1] The privilege of imposing such taxes was granted by the legislature in Connecticut. Thirty-one towns received this privilege in the years 1774–1780. See Public Records of the State of Connecticut, Vols. XIV–XVIII.

The next step was to lay out ways of communication from town to town.[1] It was difficult to secure co-operation between the autonomous local governments in this matter, the result being that such roads were often neglected.[2] Hence it became necessary to pass laws providing that new highways from town to town should be laid out, or old ways altered, by a jury appointed by the county court.[3] In case the towns to be thus connected lay in different counties, a special act of legislature was necessary, appointing a committee to do the work.[4] This method was not only cumbersome and expensive but often unsatisfactory.[5] In Connecticut, as early as 1750 these methods had to some extent been replaced by immediate action of the legislature in appointing committees to lay out more direct routes between towns in distant parts of the state between which there was considerable travel.[6]

When the routes had been determined by one or another of these methods, a narrow track was cleared of trees and rocks (in newer towns the stumps were often left standing in the road), and the logs were drawn away to furnish material for causeways and bridges.[7] Thus the roads were made passable for travelers on horseback and for ox-carts. The methods of repairing were equally simple. A contributor to the collections of the Massachusetts Historical Society from Holliston, in Middlesex County, about twenty-five miles from

[1] Dwight outlines the steps in the laying out of roads in his Travels, II. 121–122.

[2] See Public Records of Colony of Connecticut. 1684. Vol. III., p. 157.

[3] The original provision for this action is found in the Colonial Records of Connecticut, IV. 314–316, and in Massachusetts Bay, A. and R. 1693–1694. Ch. 6. A later act somewhat simplifying this process is found in the same, 1756-1757, Ch. 18.

[4] See Col. Rec. Conn. X. 107. (1752.)

[5] As in the case of the town of Woodbury which was required to keep in repair three parallel roads laid out at different times by the Litchfield county court between the towns of Litchfield and Bethlehem. Resolves and Private Laws of Connecticut, 1789–1836. Hartford. 1837. p. 607.

[6] As between Hartford and New Haven, New Haven and New London, New Haven and Windham. The most famous of these early "state roads" was that leading from Hartford through Simsbury, New Hartford, Canaan and Norfolk towards Albany, called the Greenwoods Road. In all of these cases there was no appropriation of state money for this purpose, but the towns through which the route lay were ordered to make and repair the road. This, however, they regularly failed to do. So in the case of the Greenwoods Road; although laid out in 1759 it was not constructed until 1764 and in 1766 was in "great want of amendment." Col. Rec. Conn. Vols. XI and XII.

[7] Belknap, History of New Hampshire, III. 375–378, describes in detail the clearing of new roads.

Boston, thus described the system in vogue: " . . . . the
stones, which for years had been thrown out of the way against the
walls, are thrown back, each side of the way is ploughed, the stones
are covered with dirt and the middle of the road is left the highest."[1]
Roads so constructed and so repaired were bound to be deep with
sand in summer and equally deep with mud in the fall and spring.
It is no wonder that travelers complained bitterly of them.[2]

Means of Conveyance.

The primitive sort of conveyances used at this time is perhaps
the best commentary on the state of the roads. The farmer did
his errands, and sometimes carried his produce to the country store
or his grain to the mill, on horseback. The doctor, lawyer and
minister made their professional visits in the same way. Except
between towns and cities where stage-coach routes had been established,[3] journeys both long and short were made in the saddle. For
the transportation of bulky produce, ox-carts of a construction substantial enough to defy the worst roads were employed. Chaises
with two wheels had been introduced in some towns about the middle of the eighteenth century, but four-wheeled wagons did not make

[1] Series I. Vol. 3, p. 18.

[2] A traveler from Providence, R. I., to Pomfret, Conn., wrote: "In May, 1776,
I went to Pomfret, thirty-six miles in a chaise; the road was so stony and rough,
that I could not ride out of a slow walk, but very little of the way; I was near two
days in going, such was the general state of our roads at that time." Quoted in
Field, Edward. The Colonial Tavern. p. 281.

[3] Stage-coaches began to run regularly between Boston and the larger towns
in eastern New England, especially along the coast, about 1760, and between
Boston and New York some ten or twelve years later. Passengers and a small
amount of personal baggage, and later, after the establishment of the Federal
Post Office in 1782, the mails also were transported in this way. The establishment of these lines must have led to the improvement of the roads over which
they passed and later they probably stimulated the building of turnpikes. Otherwise they had little effect upon internal trade.

An instance of the connection between the rise of the stage-coach business and
the building of turnpike roads is found in the case of Captain Pease, a pioneer
stage-coach driver and owner, who began a line from Boston to Hartford in 1783.
Of him a historian of Shrewsbury, Mass., writes: "His long career as a stage driver
gave him abundant cause to realize the bad state of the roads and the necessity
for better ones. After long and earnest efforts he procured from the Government the first charter granted in the State for a turnpike, and it was laid out in
1808 from Boston to Worcester through South Shrewsbury . . . He lived
to see it completed and to see the benefit it was to the public." Ward, Eliza-
beth. Old Times in Shrewsbury. New York. 1892. p. 55.

their appearance until about fifty years later. They were still objects of curiosity at the time of the War of 1812.[1]

The Building of Turnpike Roads.

Dissatisfaction with the existing condition of the highways, and with the administrative system outlined above, led in the years 1790–1810 to the building of turnpike roads by individuals incorporated into associations by state charters. The old roads needed repairing; new roads were needed in the newly settled communities in western Connecticut and Massachusetts. The older towns, with the antipathy to paying taxes which had become traditional, were unwilling to burden themselves with the expense of putting the roads into good condition; the new towns were unable.[2] Hence they readily adopted the turnpike scheme as a means of getting better roads without resorting to taxation. In reality they were but reviving a medieval practice in public finance, substituting a fee for a tax. That is, they restored the principle of laying the burden of an expense which was or should have been incurred for the benefit of the whole community, upon those particular individuals in the community who benefited most by it. The states turned over to the new companies certain stretches of the highways to be improved and, to reimburse them for this expense, granted them the privilege for a term of years of collecting tolls from live stock, vehicles and pedestrians at toll-gates. The charters did not specify with any great exactness what sort of a road should be constructed, but were very specific as to the number and location of the toll-gates and the tolls that should be charged.

It seemed to be a splendid scheme from all points of view. The community would get improved roads at the expense of trifling fees paid by the users, and when after a term of years the gates had been abolished the roads would still be there, and presumably the community would then find itself able to maintain them. The incorporators would, in the meanwhile, have invested their capital profitably. So attractive did this plan seem that within a few years after the first companies were chartered, agitation for turnpike build-

[1] See Felt, Joseph. History of Ipswich, Essex and Hamilton (Mass.) Cambridge, 1834. p. 32. Miss Larned tells of the introduction of these novel vehicles in Windham, Conn., in 1809. See also Wood, S. G. Taverns and Turnpikes of Blanford. Published by the author. 1908. pp. 259–261.

[2] See Miller, Edward, and Wells, Frederic P. History of Ryegate, Vermont. St. Johnsbury (Vermont). 1913. p. 148.

ing began in almost every town. In the years 1803–1807, fifty companies were chartered in Connecticut, sixty in Massachusetts and nine in Rhode Island.[1] Before 1810 there had been 180 companies organized in New England, of which 26 were in Vermont and 20 in New Hampshire.[2]

The Effect of Turnpike Roads on Inland Trade.

The turnpike companies on the whole, however, must be regarded as a failure to solve the transportation problem. In the first place, capital was not readily forthcoming for the new ventures and many of them were unable to begin construction and so forfeited their charters. Others began work but were unable to finish and their charters were renewed from time to time until they, too, finally became defunct. Many companies were organized by unscrupulous promoters, who hoped to make money out of the speculative mania which had arisen.[3] Nor were the roads which were in fact constructed under this system any great improvement over those which had formerly existed. In new districts where the only roads had been winding cartpaths through the woods, the turnpike companies did bring a real benefit, performing tasks which the sparsely settled communities would not have been able adequately to perform. But in the older towns the best that they were able to accomplish seems to have been a straightening of the roads between the larger towns. One of the old turnpike roads can even now be recognized by the direct manner in which it proceeds to its goal, uphill and down. This straightening, which was almost always accomplished at the expense of steeper grades, was not undertaken for the sake of cheapening transportation. Those engaged in carting heavy loads would have much preferred the older winding ways. But for the turnpike companies the straighter road was more profitable, because shorter. The expenditure of capital was but little greater per mile on a hilly than on a level road. The work consisted principally in clearing away stones and trees, building bridges and culverts, and digging ditches at either side of the road. The material thus secured was thrown into the middle of the road to make a crowned surface;

[1] The figures for Connecticut are from Gallatin's Report on Roads and Canals, p. 55; for Massachusetts from Private and Special Statutes of Mass., Vols. II. and III.; for Rhode Island from Index to Acts and Resolves (Rhode Island). 1758–1850.

[2] Macmaster, History of U. S. III. 463.

[3] Kendall, Travels, I. 97, explains the frequency of turnpike companies in Middlesex County, Conn., on this ground.

thus, it was hoped, drainage would be provided for. This hope was bound to be disappointed, however, as can be proven by observation of roads in outlying country districts in New England today where similar practices are followed. In none of these early turnpikes, with the exception of a few between Boston and the coast towns of Massachusetts, was any other surfacing material used besides the natural soil of the region through which they passed.[1]

In the light of such evidence as is available, it seems impossible to ascribe to the turnpike movement in the years before 1810 any significant improvement in the methods of land transportation in southern New England, or any considerable reduction in the cost of land carriage. It was still prohibitorily expensive to move bulky commodities for any distance beyond the borders of the inland town. For many of the articles of farm production a distance of from ten to twenty miles was the limit of profitable transportation;[2] beyond this limit a few products such as cheese,[3] butter, potash, maple sugar, live stock, and, in some cases, salted beef and pork, could be carried; but even in these cases the expense of carriage absorbed a large share of the profit gained.

[1] The turnpikes in Massachusetts were, on the whole, better constructed than those in Connecticut. Exceptionally good roads were those leading from Boston to Salem, Newburyport and Providence. These were surfaced with gravel, or with crushed stone, and cost to construct from $3,000 to $14,000 per mile. In Connecticut there were in 1807, 770 miles of the ordinary type of turnpike road, costing on the average from $500 to $1,000 per mile. The most expensive turnpike in this state was that from Hartford to New Haven, a distance of 35 miles, costing, including sums spent in purchasing land, $2,280 per mile. Gallatin, Report on Roads and Canals, pp. 55–56.

[2] This estimate is based on bits of scattered evidence, such as the following statement of the Rev. Samuel Goodrich in his Statistical Account of Ridgefield in the County of Fairfield (Conn.): "Potatoes are very much used and increased attempts are making to raise them for the market, but the distance from the market is so great that it is not expected the practice will be general." The distance referred to as "too great" was fourteen miles, to Norwalk. MS. in library of the Connecticut Historical Society, Hartford, Conn. In a letter from Robert Fulton contained in Gallatin's Report on Roads and Canals, there are various estimates of the cost of transportation of various commodities on the best turnpikes. These estimates vary from 10 to 30 cents per ton mile. At this rate wood could not bear the cost of transport over twenty miles. Op. cit., pp. 111, 116–117. See also Macmaster, History of U. S., III. 464.

[3] Cheese at this time sold at $160 a ton and butter at twice that price. See Statistical Account of Litchfield, Conn., p. 122.

The Insignificance of Internal Trade.

From this survey of the conditions of internal trade, we are brought to the conclusion that the opportunities to supply the markets which existed at this time, both in the commercial towns and outside New England, must have been restricted to a small proportion of the towns. The especially favored localities were, (1) a narrow strip of territory along the coast of these three states, (2) a strip of territory on both sides of the Connecticut River, (3) a few towns in Litchfield and Berkshire Counties in which cheese and other dairy products and wheat could be profitably grown, and (4) a few towns in the immediate vicinity of such ports as New Haven, Norwich, Providence and Boston.[1] Altogether these towns contained from one-fifth to one-fourth of the total population of these three states. This represents the maximum number to whom the market, such as it was, was at all accessible. The remaining portion of the agricultural population was almost entirely isolated from commercial relations with the outside world.

This fact of isolation more than any other condition or circumstance was effective in determining the economic life of the agricultural population in the inland towns of southern New England at this time. There were, it is true, many other features of the environment, in both its physical and institutional aspects, such as the soil and climate, the political and ecclesiastical systems, to which some of the most unique characteristics of the society may be ascribed. But in the background, working sometimes in harmony and sometimes in opposition to these other factors, was the predominant influence of commercial isolation.

With this chapter the analysis of the economic conditions of the life of the agricultural population is concluded. The main facts of the environment of the inland farmer are now before us. Our final task is to describe his efforts to adapt himself to that environment. In the two chapters following this process of adaptation will be outlined, first as regards the agricultural industry and then as regards the salient features of home and community life.

---

[1] The trade of the coast and river towns has already been discussed (supra, Chapter III). References to the export of agricultural products from other regions will be found in the two chapters following.

CHAPTER V.

The Agricultural Industry.

Although agriculture was the chief means whereby more than 90 per cent of the inhabitants of southern New England got their living, yet it was most inefficiently, and, to all appearances, carelessly conducted. Very little improvement had been made over the primitive methods employed by the earliest settlers. As soon as the pioneer stage had been passed and the clearing of the land had been accomplished, the colonists settled down to a routine husbandry, based largely on the knowledge and practices of English farmers of the early seventeenth century, but in many ways much less advanced than the agriculture of the motherland even at that early date. In the century and a half intervening between the settlement of New England and the opening of the nineteenth century, improvements of far-reaching significance had been introduced in English agriculture, through the work of Tull, Bakewell, Townshend, Coke, and Arthur Young. The knowledge of these changes had spread quickly to this side of the Atlantic,[1] and yet the bulk of the farmers had shown no disposition to adopt the new methods. On their poorly cultivated fields little fertilizer of any sort was used, their implements were rough and clumsy, live stock was neglected, and the same grains and vegetables were raised year after year with little attempt at a rotation of crops, until the land was exhausted.

Contemporary Criticism.

The apparent lack of intelligence, and of any progressive spirit, exhibited by the New England farmers drew severe comment from both native and foreign observers. General Warren of Massachusetts,[2] for example, writing in the American Museum in 1786, drew a sharp contrast between the methods prevailing at home and in

[1] See infra, pp. 346–347.
[2] The author of this letter was probably James Warren, 1726–1808, of Plymouth, Mass. He succeeded General Joseph Warren as president of the Provincial Congress, after the latter's death at Bunker Hill, fought through the Revolution, and was later made a major-general of militia. See Appleton's Encyclopedia of American Biography, VI. 364.

England. He says: "A man in England that farms 150 acres, would think a stock of £500 sterling necessary; three teams would be employed; four or five ploughs; barrows, wagons, carts, &c. in proportion; 70 to 80 acres tilled; 8 or 10 labourers at work; 800 to 1000 loads of manure annually collected; and perhaps three times more cattle, sheep, and hogs kept, than are kept here on a farm that is naturally as good. A man in America that farms 150 acres, would think a stock of £150 sufficient. One miserable team; a paltry plough, and everything in the same proportion; three acres of Indian corn, which require all the manure he has; as many acres of half-starved English grain from a half-cultivated soil, with a spot of potatoes, and a small yard of turneps, complete the round of his tillage, and the whole is conducted, perhaps, by a man and a boy, and performed in half their time; no manure but dung from the barn, which, if the heaps are not exposed to be washed away by the winter rains, may amount to 15 or 20 loads; and if they are so exposed to much less, without any regret to the farmer. All the rest of the farm is allotted for feeding a small stock. A large space must be mowed for a little hay for winter; and a large range for a little feed in summer. Pastures are never manured, and mowing lands seldom; . . . ."[1]

The author of American Husbandry wrote: "And the mention of cattle leads me to observe, that most of the farmers in this country are, in whatever concerns cattle, the most negligent ignorant set of men in the world . . . . Horses are in general, even valuable ones, worked hard and starved: . . . . This bad treatment extends to draft oxen; to their cows, sheep and swine; only in a different manner as may be supposed . . . .

I must, in the next place take notice of their tillage, as being weakly and insufficiently given; worse ploughing is no where to be seen, yet the farmers get tolerable crops; this is owing, particularly in new settlements, to the looseness and fertility of old woodlands which, with very bad tillage, will yield excellent crops; a circumstance the rest of the province is too apt to be guided by, for seeing the effects, they are apt to suppose the same treatment will do on land long since broken up, which is far from being the case.[2] Thus, in most parts of the province, is found shallow and unlevel furrows, which rather scratch than turn the land; and of this bad tillage the

[1] Vol. II. No. II. August, 1787. p. 347.
[2] For a further consideration of the effect of the frontier, a nearby region of new, cheap land, see infra pp. 350–352.

farmers are very sparing, rarely giving two ploughings if they think the crop will do with one; the consequence of which is their products being seldom near so great as they would be under a different management."[1]

Although usually resentful of foreign criticisms, Dwight is forced to admit that "the husbandry of New England is far inferior to that of Great Britain." He adds: "The principal defects in our husbandry, so far as I am able to judge, are a deficiency in the quantity of labour necessary to prepare the ground for seed, insufficient manuring, the want of a good rotation of crops, and slovenliness in clearing the ground. The soil is not sufficiently pulverized nor sufficiently manured. We are generally ignorant of what crops will best succeed each other, and our fields are covered with a rank growth of weeds."[2]

Farm Management in 1800.

Postponing for the present an examination of the reasons for this inefficiency in the fundamental occupation, let us examine the routine operations of the farmer in the inland communities, in order to determine as nearly as possible how far these criticisms were justified.

Size of Farms.

The 100 to 200 acres which composed a typical inland farm[3] were divided into three roughly equal tracts, one-third being woodland, including wasteland, one-third pasturage, and the remainder divided between mowing lands and cultivated fields in varying proportions. The land under tillage, however, hardly ever exceeded ten or a dozen acres, except in the neighborhood of such commercial towns as would

[1] Op. cit., I. pp. 80–81.

[2] Travels, I. 81, 82.

[3] On the matter of the prevailing size of farms there is an abundance of evidence. See Dickinson, Geographical and Statistical View, p. 7; Livingston, Robert R., American Agriculture. Article in the Edinburgh Encyclopedia. First American edition. 18 vols. Philadelphia. 1832. Vol. I. pp. 332–341. The facts in this article apply particularly to the Northern and Eastern states; many of them are taken without credit from Dickinson's work. This article was written shortly before the author's death in 1813. See De Peyster, Frederick. Biographical Sketch. New York. 1876. p. 13. The advertisements of farms for sale in the columns of the Massachusetts Spy (Worcester) in the year 1807–1808 show variations in acreage from 50 to 275 acres. But of the total of 24 farms advertised, only four had below 100 acres; 18 were between 100 and 200 acres, and only two had more than 200 acres.

furnish a market.[1] These fields were separated originally by rail fences or stone walls. In places where timber was beginning to be scarce the latter material was most generally used. When the farmer and his sons piled up these monuments of laborious toil they were accomplishing a double purpose, not only marking off the boundaries of their fields, but ridding their land of a great hindrance to cultivation as well.

The Importance of Indian Corn.

Indian corn and rye were the staple grains cultivated on every inland farm. The first might have been called the cornerstone of New England agriculture. Next to grass its yield was more valuable than that of any other crop. Dickinson says of this crop: "Indian corn may justly be considered as our principal grain, and the most valuable in the whole circle of husbandry. Its increase, compared with that of any other grain, is in a greater degree independent of the season, and governed more by the attention and care of the cultivator. It is mixed in the proportion of one-third, with rye, and constitutes the common bread of the inhabitants. The beef, pork, and poultry, fattened with it, are greatly superior to such as are fed on any other grain. Besides the crop, the average of which is about twenty-eight bushels per acre, the forage it affords is very considerable, every part of the stem and husk being applicable to the feeding of cattle."[2] Dwight says that this crop is "nearly as valuable to this country as all other kinds of corn united, and yields a crop much more certain, and much more extensively useful than any other."[3] Besides its advantage of hardiness which made

[1] According to the answers received by the Massachusetts Agricultural Society to their questionnaire of 1806, the farms in Brookfield, an exceptionally prosperous inland town in Worcester County, were divided as follows: Pasture, 33 acres; mowing, 20 acres; tillage, 6 to 7 acres; orchards, 3 to 4 acres; and woodland, 33 acres. A considerable contrast is seen in the case of Brooklyn (now called Brookline), a town adjacent to Boston, which benefited by the market in that place. Here we find a typical farm with 100 acres, of which 12 were in woodland, 20 in pasture, and 68 in mowing, tillage, and orchards. Papers, Vol. II., 1807. pp. 11, 12.

[2] Geographical and Statistical View, pp. 8–9.

[3] Travels, II. 62. In another passage, II. 294, Dwight catalogues and describes ten varieties of maize grown in New England. Other writers who recognized the importance of maize in the agricultural economy of New England were the author of American Husbandry, who calls it "the grand product of the country on which the inhabitants principally feed," I. 50, and Livingston, American Agriculture, pp. 334–335.

it surely dependable,[1] and its general utility to man and beast, this crop was peculiarly adapted to a region in which labor was expensive. The system of planting in hills at the corners of a four or five-foot square, which the colonists had learned from the Indians, rendered cultivation by cross-plowing feasible and so reduced the necessity of hand hoeing.[2] This is probably the reason why this crop was given more careful cultivation than any other. Besides rye which, combined with Indian corn, furnished the flour for bread, oats, barley, and buckwheat were regularly sown in small amounts. Both the oats and barley were recognized to be poor crops,[3] but still they were necessary, and therefore, under the self-sufficing system of agriculture, they had to be grown. The buckwheat was a useful crop in many ways. Its value in cleaning the fields of weeds was already recognized and it was also occasionally ploughed under to serve as a "green" fertilizer. The blossoms furnished food for the farmer's bees and the grain was used as a food for poultry.[4]

Why the Wheat Crop Failed.

Wheat could not be successfully grown except in a few favored regions in New England, such as the valley of the Connecticut River and the western portions of Massachusetts and Connecticut, in Berkshire and Litchfield Counties.[5] Other grains, as we shall see, yielded poor enough results, but the results of wheat cultivation were so disappointing that it was early abandoned in most regions

[1] In the answers received from the farmers in reply to its questions, the Massachusetts Society for Promoting Agriculture printed the following: "From Worcester, it is remarked, that the crop of Indian corn is the most uniform, and the one on which the farmer can most securely rely; and it is alleged, that it is the only one well cultivated in our country, and that for all these and other reasons it is thought the most useful." Papers, II. 18.

[2] See Livingston, American Agriculture, p. 335. He says further: "Ten acres of corn are hoed with less expense, than one of beans or turnips, . . ." The practice of sowing pumpkins in among the rows of corn, to which this writer in another passage refers, would have interfered somewhat with the cultivation of the corn.

[3] Of oats and barley the author of Notes on Farming says, p. 18: "I have not mentioned oats, because in this country it is a contemptible crop and scarce worth raising; barley being far better even for the feed of horses." The author of this thirty-eight page pamphlet, printed anonymously in New York in 1787, was Hon. Charles Thompson, a member of the first Continental Congress and of the Philadelphia Society for Promoting Agriculture.

[4] See Livingston, American Agriculture, p. 334.

[5] Salisbury, in Litchfield County, was especially noted for the successful cultivation of this grain. Pease and Niles, Gazetteer, p. 258.

altogether. Besides suffering from the inroads of the Canada thistle and the Hessian fly, it was repeatedly damaged by a sort of fungus growth, known to the writers of that time as blast, rust or mildew. Many attempts were made to explain this last phenomenon, which, as the investigations of the Massachusetts Society for Promoting Agriculture later proved, was really caused by the use of unselected, infected seed.[1] Dwight went to work systematically to fathom the mystery and after examining and discarding such alleged causes as the character of the soil, the climate, and the "noxious effluvia" from barberry bushes, he concludes that the damage must proceed from the use of stable manure as a fertilizer. This, he believed, forced the growth of the plant too rapidly in its early stages.[2] Harriott, the English traveler, came much nearer to a correct solution of the problem. He wrote: "In some of the farther inland parts, wheat is raised; but on the sea-coast, it has never been cultivated with much success, being subject to blasts. Various reasons are assigned for this: some suppose these blasts to be occasioned by the saline vapours from the sea; but I can not agree to this, well knowing that many of the best wheats that are grown in England in quantity and quality, are from sea-marshes and lands adjoining the sea. Others attribute it to the vicinity of Barbary-bushes of the truth of which I can not speak. But the principal cause appeared to me the poverty and sandy nature of soil in general, together with exceedingly bad management."[3]

The Lack of Root Crops.

One of the greatest defects in the system of husbandry practiced in New England was the lack of root crops. Such crops, especially the turnip, were being extensively used in England as a winter food for cattle, making possible the keeping of more animals and in better condition, besides securing for the farmer a valuable addition to his supply of stable manure. The potato was, to be sure, culti-

[1] Massachusetts Agricultural Repository and Journal. Published by the Massachusetts Society for Promoting Agriculture. 10 vols. Boston, 1793–1832. Vol. V., pp. 132–150. The first two volumes of this collection include the contributions to the Society, published as annual papers. Referred to in later notes as Mass. Agric. Soc. Papers.

[2] Travels, II. 322–329. Kittredge, The Old Farmer and His Almanack, pp. 322–332, has a chapter entitled Barberries and Wheat, in which he discusses the difficulties encountered by the farmers of the period in attempting to grow this grain.

[3] Struggles through Life, II. 32–33.

vated to some extent, and principally as a food for cattle. Although indigenous in America, it seems not to have been well known until the early part of the eighteenth century.[1] By the end of the century almost every farmer cultivated from one to four or five acres of potatoes, not in a separate field but along the borders of the corn or other grain fields. Occasionally we find turnips and carrots mentioned[2] but their cultivation had not become at all general. A cheaper substitute for root crops which was used to some extent for winter fodder was the pumpkin. Planted in the hills of corn, it required no extra land to be cultivated and grew abundantly without attention. In the fall after the corn had been cut and shocked the pumpkins were easily gathered. Although they could not be preserved as long as the root crops, yet while they lasted they furnished a fairly good substitute. Hay remained throughout all this period, however, the chief winter fodder for all sorts of live stock.[3]

Flax was not a crop especially suited to New England at this time, since it required an amount of labor and fertilization inconsistent with the prevailing extensive system of cultivation. Yet flax was necessary for the production of the homespun linen and tow cloth and hence a small field, probably only a fraction of an acre, was regularly sown. A part of the flax was allowed to ripen and although this practice made the fiber less suitable for textiles, yet from the seed thus secured linseed oil was obtained. This, as we have seen, was in some regions a commercial product.[4]

The smaller vegetables, such as peas, beans, onions,[5] etc., were

[1] Belknap, History of New Hampshire, II. 37, credits the Scotch-Irish families who settled Londonderry, New Hampshire, in 1719 with the re-introduction of this plant from Europe.

[2] As in Goodrich's Statistical Account of Ridgefield, pp. 5–6.

[3] The best contemporary discussion of the methods of planting and preserving pumpkins is found in Notes on Farming, pp. 20–21. Colonel Taylor, of Virginia, considered pumpkins a much superior crop to either turnips or potatoes, in spite of the advocacy of the latter in the English treatises with which he was familiar. The results of his experiments he published in a series of essays entitled Arator. (3 ed. Baltimore, 1817), pp. 115 ff. The bulk of this work was written before 1810.

[4] Mass. Agric. Soc. Papers, II. 1807, 41–42. In Fairfield County, Connecticut, the export of flaxseed had assumed some importance, the surplus over consumption amounting to about 20,000 bushels a year. The result of this outlet was a considerable specialization in the crop. Dwight says: "A few years since (ca. 1800) more flax was raised here than in the whole of New England beside." Travels, III. 499–500.

[5] The two towns which exported onions to any extent were Wethersfield, Connecticut, and Barnstable, Massachusetts. Pease and Niles, Gazetteer, p. 9; Kendall, Travels, II. 129.

not given much attention except in the few favored regions in the neighborhood of commercial towns, where a market for such produce was at hand.[1] Gardening was much too intensive a process for the farmer at that time. Kitchen vegetables were therefore often lacking on his table, unless the women of the household could spare time from their multifarious other occupations to plant and care for a garden.[2] The farmer had, however, learned the soothing effects of nicotine and consequently often grew a small amount of tobacco. Occasional instances of its export are found even at this early date.[3]

A few unsuccessful attempts at hemp-growing had been made in the Connecticut Valley. Although there was a considerable demand for this product at the shipyards in the commercial towns, yet such intensive cultivation was required, and so much disagreeable labor in preparing the fiber for market, that the domestic supply was greatly inadequate.[4] The breweries in Boston offered a market for hops, which was supplied by the farmers in the nearby towns.[5] Hops were also grown in small amounts by some farmers for the production of home-brewed beer. None of these smaller crops had the importance to the self-sufficient farmer, nor occupied as much of his land or attention, as the grain and grass crops. New England was at this time a region in which grazing was of more importance than the cultivation of fields, and hence the latter operations were subsidiary to the former.

The Rotation of Crops.

Very little progress had been made towards developing any systematic rotation of these crops. The simplest plan was a three-

---

[1] Dickinson, for instance, speaks of the cultivation of beans to be sold for "ship stores." Geographical and Statistical View, p. 9.

[2] The editor of the Old Farmer's Almanack occasionally encouraged his readers to pay more attention to their kitchen gardens and to introduce vegetables into the bare menu of salt beef, turnip and stewed pumpkin. See Kittredge, The Old Farmer and His Almanack, pp. 84–85. Dwight gives a long list of vegetables grown in New England gardens, but fails to tell how many of them were regularly grown in any one garden. Travels, I. 18–20.

[3] See Lees, John. Journal. New York. 1768. Also Memorial History of Hartford County, Conn. (Trumbull, J. H., ed.) 2 vols. Boston. 1886. Vol. I. p. 215. Also article, Tobacco, by Shamel, A. D., in Cyclopedia of American Agriculture (Bailey, L. H., ed.), 4 vols. New York. 1910. Vol. II. p. 641.

[4] Dickinson tells of experiments with this crop in Deerfield, Mass. Geographical and Statistical View, p. 10. See also American Husbandry, I. 54.

[5] Dwight found considerable hop-growing in Tewksbury, Mass., Travels, II. 189.

year course, alternating grain, grass and fallow, a system reminding
one of the three-field agriculture of the Middle Ages. The first crop
in this case was usually maize, followed by rye, oats or barley. It
was the practice to sow one of the latter grains in the fall after the
maize crop had ripened. After this second crop had been harvested,
the ground was laid down to grass, or more regularly left to "sow
itself;" which meant simply that it was allowed to grow up to weeds,
producing the much-condemned weed-fallow. This primitive practice was varied by the extension of the alternating crops over a period
of several years each, and also by the occasional interjection of other
crops.[1] The Massachusetts Agricultural Society summarized the
answers from its correspondents on this subject as follows: "The
answers from our other correspondents agree in stating the general
succession of crops to be Indian corn and potatoes for one or two
years; then either rye, oats or spring wheat; sometimes flax and when
the land is laid down to grass, it is usually with barley. It may be
inferred from the replies that the land is usually broken up after
being in grass three or four years; and that it is usually ploughed
about three years, and then laid down as above stated."[2] There
had been practically no improvement along this line since the Revolution, for in 1775 the author of American Husbandry had written:
"They (the farmers of New England) sow large quantities of maize,
some wheat, barley, oats, buckwheat, pease, and beans, turneps,
and clover: hemp and flax in small parcels. And these they throw
after one another, with variations, so as to keep the land, as well
as their ideas permit, from being quite exhausted; which they effect
by the intervention of a ploughed summer fallow sometimes. When
the land has borne corn for several years, till it threatens to yield
no more, then they sow clover among the last crop, and leave it
as a meadow for some years to recover itself. But all this system
proceeds too much on the plan of the worst farmers of Great Britain,
to get corn (*i.e.*, grain) from their fields as long as ever they will
bear it."[3] In general we may say that some farmers were making

---

[1] According to the Rev. Mr. Goodrich, the rotation of crops practiced in Ridgefield was: 1st year, buckwheat or rye; 2nd year, Indian corn; 3rd year, flax or
oats, followed by rye sown in the fall; 4th year, pasture. After remaining in
pasture a few years the land was broken up and the same routine was repeated.
Statistical Account, p. 6.

[2] Papers, II. 28.

[3] Op. cit., pp. 75-76. Clover had been introduced in some parts, but not to
any great extent, before 1800. It was valued rather as making good hay than
for any appreciation of its service in recuperating the soil. Deane wrote in 1790:

a conscious but unsystematized effort to secure a more beneficial alternation of crops, but because of the limitations of their knowledge on the subject[1] and because of the necessity of getting certain staples, such as corn, rye, grass and flax, under any conditions, they had made practically no progress along this line.

The Neglect of Manure.

There are two means of preventing soil exhaustion and of restoring the fertility of mismanaged soils; one is by a system of scientific rotation of crops and the other is by the regular and liberal application of fertilizers. As we have seen, the farmers at this period had very little knowledge of the former method, even of an empirical nature. Although we could not expect them to understand the principles of soil chemistry, the beneficial effect of common fertilizers was so obviously apparent that their neglect of this method of enriching their soil seems at first glance astonishing. The barnyard and stable manure would, if carefully collected and preserved, have furnished a considerable supply[2] of first-class fertilizing material, but this resource was uniformly neglected. The cattle and horses were turned out to pasture early in the summer and often were not put into stables again, even for over night, until late in the fall.[3] Even the small amount of manure which accumu-

"Some think clover is so far from needing any manure, that it will recruit lands which are worn out. That it will do it more than other grasses, I cannot yet see any reason to believe. It will bear no crop worth mowing on lands which are quite exhausted. But it is probable, it may produce good crops on lands which are much impoverished near the surface, by bearing plants with short or horizontal roots; because clover sends its main roots to a great depth. And while a field lies several years in clover, the soil near the surface may be considerably recruited. But whether the land on the whole will be in better heart, after several heavy crops of clover are taken from it, and no manure laid on, seems rather doubtful." Deane, Samuel, A. M., The New England Farmer. 1 ed. Worcester. 1790. p. 60.

[1] The state of knowledge on this subject is apparent from the following: "There seems to be a general opinion that potatoes are a beneficial crop, and an universal sentiment that flax is a pernicious one. Another opinion is equally universal, that a succession of crops is absolutely essential to good cultivation, though there does not appear to have been any accurate experiments to ascertain the best order, or the duration of this rotation." Mass. Agric. Soc. Papers. II. 1807. 28.

[2] In the Papers of the Massachusetts Agricultural Society for 1807 it was estimated that the live stock ordinarily kept on a 100-acre farm would furnish about 50 cart loads of dung. pp. 42–45.

[3] General Warren wrote: "The common practice, in this country, is, in winter, when they (the cattle) are turned out of the barn, to take no further care of

lated during the winter was imperfectly protected from the weather and consequently a large proportion of it was wasted.[1]

An artificial manure, or commercial fertilizer, as it would be called nowadays, known as gypsum or Plaster of Paris, had been introduced in a few towns as early as 1800. Like other calcareous substances, it did not furnish a lacking element of plant food, yet its action was beneficial in counteracting the acidity of certain soils, and it may have also aided in retaining moisture in dry soils. The gypsum used in New England was quarried in Nova Scotia and transported hither by water. Then it had to be ground, either in plaster mills erected for that purpose, or more often, in grist mills. The cost of this process plus that of transportation and of quarrying, made this form of fertilizer so expensive that only a few farmers could afford to use it.[2] Consequently its use was confined to a few towns in sections from which crops could be exported, such as the wheat-growing regions of the western counties and in the Connecticut Valley.[3]

On the seacoast two fertilizers were easily accessible, fish and seaweed. Along the Connecticut shore of Long Island Sound, whitefish were caught in great quantities and applied to the land at the

them for the day; they are suffered to range at large in summer; it is not uncommon to bring them up in the evening, and let them lie till morning in the roads; the first rains wash the roads clear for the traveller, without any injury to the farmer, who would not have taken the trouble to have cleaned them for any other purpose; . . . ." Letter in American Museum, II. 347.

[1] European travelers could not understand why the New England farmers and those of the Eastern states in general should be so indifferent to this means of fertilization. Harriott relates, Struggles through Life, II. 216, that on the farm which he purchased on Long Island there was "some hundred loads of manure which had been accumulating for several years, to the great damage of the buildings." This accumulation was looked upon by his neighbors as an encumbrance, merely, and the former owner advised him to move his barn, as this would be an easier way out of the difficulty than moving the manure. A similar state of affairs was described by La Rochefoucauld in Lebanon, Connecticut. Travels, I. 516.

[2] Livingston, American Agriculture, p. 338, estimated the cost to the farmer at 50 cents a bushel. When we consider that the purchasing power of money was very considerably higher in those days, this price, which is about that which a farmer pays nowadays for his commercial fertilizers, seems extremely high.

[3] Kendall found gypsum costing $20 a ton in use by the farmers in Sharon, in Litchfield County. Travels, I. 231. Dwight, in the course of his travels, found gypsum in use in nine towns in New England. It is significant that eight of these towns are in the Connecticut Valley. The ninth, Plainfield, Connecticut, profited by the outlet for surplus products furnished by the port of Norwich.

rate of 10,000 to 12,000 per acre.[1] Seaweed, or rock-weed as it was called, was easily collected and served the same purpose to a less degree. Both at the shore and inland a variety of other fertilizing agents was used, such as marl, potash and lime, but only sporadically, according to the enterprise of particular farmers and the accessibility of the material.

The prevailing neglect of fertilizers, to which the occasional use of gypsum and white-fish are merely exceptions, illustrates not so much the ignorance of the typical farmer, as the inhibitory effect of the lack of a market on all progress in the science of agriculture. Of course the farmers of that day did not understand why spreading the dung of their cattle on their fields increased the yield of their crops, but they knew very well that such was in fact the result. Even if they had had more knowledge, it is not likely that they would have modified their wasteful practice. For carting and spreading manure entailed labor, which meant expense either of money or of their own physical effort. And from what source was that expense to be repaid? Not, certainly, from the sale of crops, for without a market that was impossible. The old practices resulted in crops sufficient to feed the farmer and his family. Why should he exert himself to produce a surplus? The only return he could expect would be a sort of psychological income, a satisfaction in seeing his fields yielding more than those of his neighbors. Such satisfaction was a quite sufficient stimulus for the gentleman farmer of the commercial towns, who experimented along all sorts of lines, regardless of expense, but for the self-sufficient farmer it

[1] Dwight noted the use of white-fish in Branford, Killingworth, and Guilford. Of the latter town he remarks: "The soil of East Guilford is naturally less rich than that on which the town is built; but, being extensively manured with white-fish, yields abundant crops. These fish are sometimes laid in furrows, and covered with the plough. Sometimes they are laid singly on the hills of maize and covered with the hoe. At other times they are collected in heaps, formed with other materials into a compost, carted upon the ground, and spread in the same manner, as manure from the stable. A single net has taken 200,000 in a day. They are sold for a dollar a thousand, and are said to affect the soil advantageously for a considerable length of time. The people of East Guilford are not a little indebted to them for their present prosperity."

This prosperity, however, had its drawbacks. Dwight continues with conscientious adherence to detail: "One very disagreeable circumstance attends this mode of husbandry. At the season, when the white-fish are caught in the greatest quantities, an almost intolerable foetor fills the surrounding atmosphere, and however use may have reconciled it to the senses of the inhabitants, it is extremely disgusting to a traveller." Travels, II. 491–492.

was a psychological luxury in which he did not feel he could afford to indulge. The farmers of Litchfield and Berkshire and of the Connecticut Valley had no more knowledge of the scientific principles involved in the action of gypsum as a fertilizer than had their contemporaries in the hills of Worcester or Tolland, but they had learned somehow that gypsum produced bigger crops. They wanted bigger crops because they had a market. Hence they were willing to invest their money and labor and make the experiment. Hence their progress in the science of agriculture.

The Farm Equipment—Buildings, Tools and Implements.

It was this lack of a market which explains to a large extent the small investment of capital in agriculture at this time, either in permanent improvements, such as drains and buildings, or in tools and implements. A house and barn were necessary and these were in general conveniently and substantially built. The latter had a threshing floor in the middle and stables for horses and cows on either side. Some of the hay was mowed away above the stables and the remainder was stacked near the barn in sheds, open at the sides and covered with a thatched or shingled roof. A corn-crib was always in evidence, set up on stilts as now, as a protection against mice and dampness. Of the tools and implements used on the farm we shall have occasion to speak in another connection.[1] They were few and ill-contrived. One writer says that the farmer of this period could have carried them all, except the cart and harrow, upon his back.[2] They included a plough, a hoe, a pitchfork, a manure-fork and a shovel, all of which were clumsily constructed of wood, often by the farmer himself, and plated with strips of sheet iron, perhaps by the local blacksmith; a flail for threshing grain and a a fan and riddle-sieve for winnowing. The practice of treading out the grain from the straw by driving cattle over it, which had persisted since the days of the ancient Israelites, was still to be found in some of the Middle states, but seems to have been superseded in New England.[3] The sickle, the most ancient of harvesting im-

[1] See infra, pp. 364–365.

[2] Flint, Charles Louis. Progress in Agriculture. In Eighty Years' Progress of the United States. Hartford. 1867. p. 24.

[3] See American Museum, V. 379; and Deane, New England Farmer, p. 283. A day's work with the flail yielded from four to six bushels of wheat and from six to twelve bushels of barley, according to the size of the grains. Ibid. Indian corn was sometimes threshed with a flail but a more efficient method was to scrape the grains from the cob by rubbing the ear across the edge of a spade. Mass. Agric. Soc. Papers, II. 1807, 25–26.

plements, was still used to some extent in reaping wheat; for cutting other grains and grass, the scythe and cradle were used.[1]

For the all-important business of ploughing the farmer was but poorly equipped. Flint has given us a description of two of the types of ploughs most frequently used at this time. He says: "The Carey plough had a clumsy wrought-iron share, a land-side and standard made of wood, a wooden mould-board, often plated over in a rough manner with pieces of old saw-plates, tin or sheet-iron. The handles were upright, and were held by two pins; a powerful man was required to hold it, and double the strength of team now commonly used in doing the same kind of work. The 'bar-side plough' or the 'bull plough' was also used to some extent. A flat bar formed the land-side, and a big clump of iron, shaped a little like the half of a lance head, served as a point, into the upper part of which a kind of coulter was fastened. The mould-board was wooden and fitted to the irons in the most bungling manner. The action might be illustrated by holding a sharp-pointed shovel back up, and thrusting it through the ground."[2] With such unwieldly instruments, two men or a man and a boy, using three horses or two or three yoke of oxen, could turn over in a superficial manner the soil of one or two acres in a day.[3] Some attempts had been made to improve this implement; a cast-iron plough had been invented in 1797 in which the mold-board and land-side were cast in one piece,[4] but the mass of the farmers were ignorant of these improvements. The iron plough was even opposed because of the fear that it would poison the earth.

Harrows were used to further pulverize the soil. These had at times iron, but probably more usually wooden teeth. Of the latter Deane says: " . . . they are of so little advantage to the land, unless it be merely for covering seeds, that they may be considered as unfit to be used at all. The treading of the cattle that draw them, will harden the soil more, perhaps, than these harrows will soften it."[5] All the transportation of crops, manure, timber and

---

[1] The inefficiency of these tools appears in the following figures: Using a sickle, a man could cut one acre of wheat in a day; with a cradle he could cut four acres of oats or barley, and with a scythe, one acre of green grass. Deane, New England Farmer, p. 380.

[2] Eighty Years' Progress, pp. 27–28. See also American Husbandry, I. 81–82.

[3] American Museum, V. 379–380.

[4] By Charles Newbold, of New Jersey. See Carver, T. N., Historical Sketch of American Agriculture in Bailey's Cyclopedia of American Agriculture. IV. 56.

[5] New England Farmer. (2 ed.) p. 142.

stone was done, except when there was snow on the ground, by means of ox-carts, ponderous two-wheeled vehicles, constructed almost entirely of wood. The carriage of goods for any distance was, if possible, postponed until winter when sledges or sleighs could be used.

The Yield per Acre of Various Crops.

The best method of determining just how inefficient was the practice of husbandry outlined in the foregoing paragraphs, would seem to be an examination of the yield of the various crops cultivated. There are, of course, no government reports going back to those early days[1] nor are there any other official publications covering this period. There exists, however, a considerable mass of information on this point scattered through the various gazetteers and statistical accounts of towns and in the writings of travelers. This material refers to conditions in various parts of southern New England, in general between the years 1790–1810. The following figures have been compiled from a digest of such scattered information, making allowance for exceptional conditions in certain localities which would cause variations from the normal figures. Indian corn produced on an average 25 to 30 bushels per acre. Occasionally crops of as high as 40 or 50 bushels were recorded, in the Connecticut Valley, and, on the other hand, on sandy soil such as that of Cape Cod and of Nantucket the yield fell to 12 bushels per acre or less. Rye was considerably less prolific, averaging about 15 bushels per acre. This crop was curiously uniform over the entire area, hardly any cases being found where crops larger than this were harvested, and only occasionally did the yield fall to 12 or 10 bushels. Potatoes are credited with 100 to 150 bushels per acre, a figure which compares very favorably with those of the latest censuses,[2] but this is probably due to inaccuracy at the earlier date in estimating the crop, since, as we have seen, potatoes were rarely grown by themselves in fields of any considerable size. Barley produced about 20 bushels to the acre, and buckwheat from 15 to 20 bushels. The yield of wheat, in the limited areas in which it was cultivated, was miserably low, hardly ever rising above 15 bushels to the acre, and averaging between 10 and 15.[3]

[1] The census of 1840 was the first in which agricultural statistics were collected.

[2] In 1909 the yield for New England averaged 176.9 bushels per acre; in 1899 it was 130.3. U. S. Bureau of the Census. Thirteenth Census. 1910. Abstract. p. 399.

[3] For the best collation of figures for crop yields in any single work see Mass. Agric. Soc. Papers, II. 1807, 14–19.

The Apple Orchard.

Apples were the standard fruit of New England. As we have seen, every farm had an orchard of several acres, containing a hundred or more trees.[1] The abundant yield of these trees seems to have been used principally for making cider, the favorite beverage of all classes and persons.[2] Some was exported to the Southern states, either in its natural form or after being distilled into cider brandy, but the bulk of the product was stored away in the farmers' cellars for their own consumption. Apples were also preserved by slicing and drying for winter use in the household. In especially fruitful years there was still a surplus, which was fed to the cattle and swine. Other orchard fruits of less importance were pears, peaches, plums, cherries and quinces. The orchards suffered much from the lack of care. After the original planting, practically nothing was done to preserve the trees or increase their yield except to allow cattle to pasture among them and, very rarely, to plough between the trees. The result of this neglect was becoming apparent at the beginning of the century. The first growth of orchards in many towns was dying out and often the trees were so infested with worms that the value of their fruit was largely destroyed.[3]

The Management of Woodland.

Every farm had also its woodland, occupying perhaps one-third of its total area, and every farmer was to some extent a lumberman and forester. The importance of wood in the farm economy we have already noted. Houses and barns, tools and vehicles, furniture and utensils, were constructed of this material to a much greater

---

[1] In the advertisements of farms for sale in the newspapers of the day great stress was laid on the capacity of the orchards as cider producers. For instance, a farm of 270 acres in Coventry, Connecticut, had an orchard capable of producing 60–100 barrels of cider annually. Windham Herald, January 11, 1811.

[2] As an instance of the popularity of this beverage Miss Earle relates that cider, diluted with water, was drunk by children when milk was scarce. It was also supplied in large amounts to college students. Home Life in Colonial Days. New York. 1898. pp. 148–149, 161–162. Charles Francis Adams writes: "Later, (*i.e.*, after the early years of colonial life) cider seems to have supplanted beer as the every-day and all-day beverage, and the quantity of it drunk by all classes down to a late period in this century was almost incredible. In the cellars of the more well-to-do houses a barrel of cider was always on tap, and pitchers of it were brought up at every meal, and in the morning and evening." Episodes. II. 686.

[3] Travelers commented on the poor condition of the orchards throughout southern New England. See Harriott, Struggles through Life, II. 34–35; Kendall, Travels, III. 35; Brissot de Warville, New Travels, p. 132.

extent than now. Besides this, the consumption of wood for fuel was enormous. The open fire-places demanded constant replenishing during the winter months and consequently the wood-pile formed an imposing eminence behind every farmhouse. In their wholesale and seemingly reckless destruction of timber in clearing the land, the settlers seem not to have anticipated the subsequent importance of this material to them.[1] As a result of their improvidence there seems to have been in 1810 little first-growth timber standing, except in the more lately settled counties of western Massachusetts and Connecticut.[2] And even in the management of such woodland as they had, the farmers of this period followed a bad system. The policy was to cut off close a certain tract every year, depending on the natural growth to replace it after a term of years. The better method, that of selecting certain trees over the whole extent of the woodland to be cut every year, was discarded because of the larger amount of labor which would have been necessary in gathering the wood. Ignorance of the better policy may also have been responsible.[3] The scarcity of wood,[4] which was inevitable, had begun to be felt, especially in the matter of fuel. In regions of naturally sparse forestation, as on Cape Cod, fire-wood was imported and experiments were being made with the use of peat as fuel.[5]

[1] The author of American Husbandry severely condemned this waste and seems to have anticipated to some extent the modern conservation movement in advocating legislative restraint. Op. cit., I. 84. See also Whitney, History of the County of Worcester, p. 249; and Belknap, History of New Hampshire, III. 26.

[2] Dickinson, Geographical and Statistical View, p. 9, describes the forests still existing in Massachusetts, ca. 1810.

[3] There seems to have been little agreement as to the time required for reforestation. See Dwight, Travels, I. 80; and Mass. Agric. Soc. Papers, II. 1807, 47.

[4] In a number of works this is given as the reason for the substitution of stone walls for rail fences. See Statistical Account of Litchfield, p. 92; Goodrich, Statistical Account of Ridgefield, p. 8.

[5] Joseph Felt wrote in 1834: "The first settlers thought no more of burning twenty or thirty cords of wood annually than we do of burning five. . . . Peat began to be used in some families about fifty years since . . . . It was made into coal sixty years past and used on the forges of blacksmiths." History of Ipswich, Essex and Hamilton. pp. 25–26. In his Observations on the Agriculture of the United States, William Strickland wrote that timber and wood had doubled in price in every part of New England within ten years. Strickland was an Englishman who spent a few months in this country as an agent of the British Board of Agriculture. He seems to have been diligent in his collection of facts, although his generalizations are colored by prejudice to some extent. The result of his work, a seventy-four page pamphlet, was published in London in 1801.

Meadows and Pastureland.

The New England region was by nature better fitted for grazing and pasturage than for agriculture in the strict sense of the word. Its soil, although of a good quality, was thin and the fields were much encumbered by stones and boulders, varying in size from small pebbles to huge rocks and ledges.[1] Hence the farmer's meadows and pasture lands tended to assume more importance than his tilled fields. The natural grass, which sprang up and grew abundantly as soon as the land was cleared, was of excellent quality.[2] On the uplands it furnished good pasturage and from the meadows, which were almost always watered by a small stream, fair crops of hay could be secured with the labor only of harvesting. Grass was also cut on the tilled lands in the years in which they were lying fallow. Occasionally these fields were seeded down with clover or with timothy, sown in with a previous grain crop. This occurred only at long intervals, however, and the seed used was not only full of impurities but was insufficient in quantity.[3] For the most part, in the intervals between its years of tillage the land was left to "seed itself." Just at the end of the period under consideration the sowing of clover seems to have spread quite rapidly. Livingston, writing in 1813, says: "The introduction of clover, . . . has within the last 10 years made a very sensible improvement in the agriculture of the country . . . . Indeed it is only within the last twenty years that any grass seed has been sown; and it will be no exaggeration to say, that more clover seed has been put in, within the last eight years, than has ever been sown since the country was inhabited."[4]

The pasturage furnished subsistence for the farmer's cattle, sheep,

[1] President Butterfield of the Massachusetts Agricultural College, has written: "It is sometimes asserted that the soil of New England is a drawback. On the contrary it is an asset. True there are many square miles . . . . consisting of ledges, others almost plastered with boulders; but wherever there is clear soil it is good soil—the very best." Art. N. E. Agriculture. In New England— What It Is and What It Is To Be. (George French, ed.) Boston. 1911. p. 115.

[2] Dwight wrote: "Grass is undoubtedly the most valuable object of culture in New England." Travels, I. 22. The excellence of the natural grass was commented upon in American Husbandry, I. 57. It was this grass which was later introduced into England, receiving the name timothy. After its re-introduction into New England it was known as English grass or spear grass.

[3] Clover was sown at the rate of about six pounds to the acre; of grass seed six quarts were used on the same area. Mass. Agric. Soc. Papers, II. 1807, 29.

[4] American Agriculture, p. 335.

and horses during the summer months;[1] the hay, supplemented to some extent with corn stalks, rye and wheat straw, and potatoes, supplied their winter fodder. Grain was rarely fed, except to hard-worked horses, or to beef cattle which were being fattened for slaughtering. A typical inland farm of 100 acres was able to support in this manner 10 or 15 cows, including young stock, one or two yoke of oxen, one or two horses, a flock of from 10 to 20 sheep and about as many swine as cows.[2]

The Native Cattle.

The beef cattle were the descendants of the Devonshire breed originally imported by the earliest settlers, but had received considerable intermixture from the Danish breed imported into New Hampshire and probably also from the Holstein breed brought by the Dutch colonists to New York. These influences, as well as lack of sufficient winter fodder and inattention to selection in breeding, had developed in New England a breed known as "the native cattle," more remarkable for their hardiness than for the production of beef or dairy products. In a few sections, however, such as in the towns of the Connecticut Valley and along the shores of Narragansett Bay,[3] where the pasturage was especially rich and a market for salted beef could be reached, some improvement in the breed was remarked.[4] The dairy products from the farmer's cows were an

[1] The most reliable writers tell us that cattle were "housed" from the beginning or the middle of November until the middle or latter part of May. The neglect of live stock in this regard, about which travelers had complained at an earlier period (see La Rochefoucauld, I. 495–496; 513), seems to have been caused not by pure inhumanity but by reluctance, perhaps inability, to invest capital in barns and sheds.

[2] These figures are taken from the answers received by the Massachusetts Agricultural Society in reply to their questions of 1806. Papers, II. 1807, 35. They agree in general with those given by Livingston, American Agriculture, p. 335. Occasionally advertisements of farms for sale in the columns of the country weekly newspapers yield information on this point. In Mansfield, Connecticut, the live stock on a farm offered for sale consisted of 10 cows, one yoke of oxen, six three-year-old steers, four two-year-old steers, two horses, 20 sheep and four hogs. Windham Herald, April 10, 1806. A Windham farm had two oxen, two two-year-old steers, five cows, five yearlings, five calves, 16 sheep and two horses. Ibid. November 3, 1808.

[3] Morse considered the cattle in the latter region the finest in New England. They would weigh, he thought, from 1,600 to 1,800 lbs. Gazetteer, 1810, art. Rhode Island.

[4] An improvement in the breeding of cattle was one of the primary objects of the Berkshire Agricultural Society, established by Elkanah Watson in Pittsfield in Berkshire County, Massachusetts, in 1810.

important article of his diet.   In cheese, moreover, an article was found for which the demand in the Southern states and in the West Indies was considerable.   Cheese had also enough value in proportion to its weight to bear the expense of transportation by land for some distance.   A few towns in Litchfield and Berkshire Counties, on the western edge of New England, and a few others in Rhode Island along Narragansett Bay, and in Windham County in Connecticut, exported large quantities of cheese and grew prosperous in consequence.[1]

Oxen and Horses.

The cattle not only supplied the farm with beef and dairy products but also furnished a part of its labor force.   Oxen were from the beginning the favorite, and, in fact for many years, the only draft animal on New England farms.   Although horses were steadily coming into more general use, they did not seriously compete with the slower-moving steers for general farm work for many years after 1810.[2]   In 1784 there were about 45,500 horses in Massachusetts and over 162,500 oxen and draft cattle.[3]   In 1792 in New Hampshire the proportion of horses to neat cattle was only one in twenty.[4]   By 1812 this ratio had increased to about one in seven.[5]   In spite of their slowness of gait the oxen had certain advantages which justified the farmers in their use.   These are succinctly set forth by President Dwight as follows: "The advantages of employing oxen are, that they will endure more fatigue, draw more steadily, and surely; are purchased for a smaller price; are kept at less expense;

[1] The town of Goshen, in Litchfield County, was noted for its cheese.   Dwight wrote of this town: "It is, perhaps, the best grazing ground in the state; and the inhabitants are probably more wealthy than any other collection of farmers in New England, equally numerous.   The quantity of cheese made by them annually, is estimated at four hundred thousand pounds weight.   Butter also is made in great quantities."   Travels, II. 355.   Pease and Niles give the amount exported from this town in 1819 as 380,266 lbs.   Gazetteer, p. 248.   A neighboring town, marketed 100 tons of cheese in 1811, besides 6 tons of butter.   Morris, Statistical Account of Litchfield, p. 122.

[2] One writer puts the date of the beginning of such competition as late as 1870. See Marquis, J. C.   An Economic History of Agriculture in New England since 1840.   Thesis submitted to the Faculty of Purdue University for the degree of Master of Science in Agriculture.   1909.   Ms. p. 148.

[3] These figures are given in the American Museum, VII. 54.

[4] Belknap, History of New Hampshire, III. 144.

[5] Merrill, Eliphalet and Phinehas, Gazetteer of the State of New Hampshire. Exeter, N. H., 1817, p. 16.   The figures are 32,000 and 211,500, respectively.

are freer from disease; suffer less from labouring on rough grounds; and perform the labour better; and, when by age or accident they become unfit for labour, they are converted into beef. The only advantage of employing horses instead of oxen, is derived from their speed."[1]

The use of horses for travel and light transportation increased rapidly with the introduction of wagons and the building of turnpike roads in the first decade of the new century, the oxen being still retained for the heavier tasks of ploughing and of hauling crops, stone and timber.[2] In fact, as Livingston points out, the typical horse of New England, the Narragansett, was much too high spirited and lightly built for farm work.[3] The horses, which were largely raised either by the farmer himself or in the vicinity,[4] had suffered the same degenerating tendency as the cattle. Dickinson wrote: "Our horses are mostly of an inferior kind. Little attention has been paid to them, and it is believed that they have rather declined within fifteen or twenty years. When one casts his eye upon the saddle horses of Virginia, or upon the draft horses of Pennsylvania, he must be strongly impressed with the great improvement of which our comparatively diminutive breed of horses is susceptible."[5]

Swine were kept on every farm, furnishing the salt-pork which was a staple article of diet. They required but little attention; in the fall they were ringed through the nose as a precaution against rooting, and turned out into the stubble fields, as gleaners after the harvest. In the winter they were fed on anything which happened to be superfluous, hay, chestnuts, apples, potatoes, dairy and kitchen

[1] Statistical Account of New Haven, p. 22. See also American Museum, II. 85; VIII. 24–25. Tudor believed thoroughly in the superior efficiency of oxen. He wrote: "An advantage to the farmer, individually, and a very important benefit in its general results, is owing to the use of oxen, instead of horses, in almost all agricultural labour." Letters on the Eastern States, p. 241.

[2] Horses and oxen had in earlier years often been used together as the following quotation shows: "Our teams used for transportation and the several branches of husbandry have been generally composed of oxen and horses together and our vehicles for carriage have been carts and sleds, but within a few years past waggons drawn by horses have greatly multiplied and the cart harrow and plow are more frequently drawn by oxen alone." Goodrich, Statistical Account of Ridgefield, p. 8.

[3] American Agriculture, p. 336.

[4] Breeding horses and mules for the West India market had become an industry of some importance in a few towns. Advertisements of stallions and Spanish jacks at stud were frequent in the newspapers in Worcester and Windham counties.

[5] Geographical and Statistical View, pp. 11–12.

refuse. For a few months before slaughtering they were fed on Indian corn. They thrived under this treatment and seem to have been the most successfully developed animals on the farm. Harriott wrote of the swine which he saw in Rhode Island: "Hogs they have as good and as large as can be bred in any part of the globe."[1] In the Newport market he observed several weighing about 600 lbs. each, and on inquiry was informed that such weight was not unusual. The average size in other regions was, however, probably considerably under this figure.[2]

Sheep of the Common Breed.

The flock of 20 or 25 sheep regularly found on every farm was a characteristic feature of the self-sufficient agriculture. So vitally important were they as the source of supply of wool[3] that in spite of the constant discouragements of colonial days,[4] the sheep had increased steadily in numbers in proportion to the growth of population. No feature of the farm economy shows more clearly than the management of sheep the neglect and want of progress which the lack of a market brought about; and on the other hand, no department of the agricultural industry responded more promptly in improvement when once the market was supplied. Up to 1800 no attempts had been made to improve the breed of sheep. They had, probably, in common with the cows and horses, degenerated since their introduction by the first settlers. They were long-legged, narrow in the breast and back, and slow in arriving at maturity. When fully grown, they yielded only 40 or 45 pounds of mutton, and about three or three and one-half pounds of coarse wool at each shearing.[5]

[1] Struggles through Life. II. 39.

[2] In the papers of the Mass. Agric. Soc., II. 1807, 38–39, the weights given are from 250 to 400 lbs. See also Belknap, History of New Hampshire, III. 245.

[3] The value of the sheep as meat producers seems to have been quite subsidiary. This was due in large part to a prejudice among the farmers against mutton as an article of diet. See U. S. Dept. of Agriculture. Special Report on the History and Present Condition of the Sheep Industry of the United States. Prepared under the direction of Dr. D. E. Salmon. Washington. 1892. 52 Cong. 2 Sess. Misc. Doc. No. 105, p. 74.

[4] Among these discouragements were the ravages of wolves and later of dogs. It was the desire to escape the former danger which first led to the pasturage of sheep on the islands in Boston Harbor and later on the larger islands of Nantucket and Martha's Vineyard. The flocks on these islands had in 1810 increased to very considerable size (supra p. 290 and note), furnishing a surplus of wool for export. See Wright, C. W., Wool Growing and the Tariff. Harvard University Economic Studies. Vol. V. Cambridge. 1910. pp. 2 ff.

[5] See Sheep Industry in U. S., p. 51; Mass. Agric. Soc. Papers, II. 1807, 38.

The Importations of Merino Sheep.

Between 1800 and 1815, a noteworthy effort was made to improve the native stock by the importation of rams and ewes from Spain. The Spanish Merino sheep had long been famous for the weight and excellent quality of their wool, but on account of rigid exportation restrictions it had been practically impossible to bring representatives of the stock to this country. These restrictions were broken down about the year 1800, during the disorganization of the government of Spain following the Napoleonic invasion. Advantage of this state of affairs was taken by our ambassadors in Spain and France, Col. David Humphreys and Robert Livingston, as well as by certain other Americans who were abroad at that time. They secured a few of these valuable animals, which they shipped back to America. The only importations of importance into New England before 1809 were the flock of 70 ewes and 21 rams sent by Col. Humphreys in 1802.[1] Although from the very first there was no doubt of the great improvement which the mixture of the Spanish with the native breed produced upon the latter,[2] yet the ordinary farmer was slow in benefiting thereby. In the first place, the knowledge of the importations spread slowly, and then the prices at which the Merinos sold were so exorbitant,[3] that few even of the most prosperous of gentlemen-farmers could afford to experiment with them. In general we may say that it was the lack of a commercial stimulus which retarded progress along this line, as well as along all others. The native breed, poor as they were, supplied enough wool and mutton for the farmer's own family.[4] The demand for wool in the domestic

[1] Sheep Industry in U. S., p. 136.

[2] The Massachusetts Agricultural Society printed in its Papers for 1807 two enthusiastic letters from Colonel Humphreys stating that the Merinos, both of pure and mixed blood, were hardier, better adapted to the climate of New England, and more easily nourished than the common or native breed. In addition they produced more and better wool and attained a larger size and greater weight. pp. 59–63.

[3] Humphreys did not sell any until 1805; then he sold some at prices ranging from $1,000 to $1,500 apiece. Livingston sold his rams at $150 apiece. Sheep Industry in U. S., pp. 140, 167.

[4] Livingston describes the position of sheep in American agriculture as follows: "Sheep have heretofore not been kept in any great numbers. They never made an object in American husbandry. Every farmer kept a few to run over his stubble, and pick up the hay that the horses and cattle wasted. There being no regular demand for wool, no more sheep were kept than supplied the farmer's family with what was necessary for their domestic manufacture of stockings, mittens, petticoats, coverlids, and coarse cloth for servants and children . . . ." American Agriculture, p. 336.

industries was, it is true, steadily increasing, but it had not become strong enough to induce a systematic attempt to improve the breed. It was not until the newly established woolen factories[1] had grown to be large consumers of wool that the New England farmers felt the impetus to increased production.

The attempts to improve the breed of sheep by the importation of the Merinos is a typical illustration of a larger movement towards the betterment of the agricultural industry as a whole, which began to make progress in the closing years of the eighteenth century. The impetus came from the patriotic impulses of men of education and of public affairs, who had come to learn of the "new husbandry" of Tull, Bakewell, and Young, which had created such a stir in England. Some of them had by personal observation been impressed with the contrast presented by the results of the improved system beside the wasteful and inefficient methods with which they were familiar at home.[2] Others, like Washington, had learned of the English improvements at second-hand but had increased their knowledge by active correspondence with the leaders of the movement on the other side.[3] The Revolution itself had its part in furthering this new movement. Not only did it arouse a new patriotism, but, in conventions as well as on the field, it brought together and made acquainted the leading men from the various states. When, after these exciting days were over, they had retired to their homes, they turned their energies to the improvement of agriculture.

The Agricultural Societies—Character of their Work.

In order to make their efforts more effective, these pioneers in agricultural improvement formed associations or agricultural societies, modeled in general upon those which had been organized abroad.[4]

[1] For a discussion of the number and size of these factories established before 1810, see supra pp. 273-274.

[2] Such pioneers in the movement for agricultural improvement as Samuel Adams, David Humphreys, Elkanah Watson, as well as Jefferson and Livingston, had all had opportunities to observe the English and European methods in the years between the Revolution and 1810.

[3] Washington corresponded with Arthur Young, William Strickland, with James Anderson, the Scottish economist and agriculturist, and with Sir John Sinclair, the first president of the British Board of Agriculture. The latter wrote numerous letters to such prominent men as James Madison, John Jay, Gouverneur Morris and James Monroe, which, it must be confessed, were on the whole neglectfully answered. See Sinclair's Correspondence. 2 vols. London. 1831, passim.

[4] The predominance of foreign influences in the establishment of these societies is clearly apparent. In the preface to the Memoirs of the Philadelphia society

The nature of these societies and of the work they proposed to carry on is clearly revealed in the prefaces of their articles of association. They were not intended to be clubs of practical working farmers who might aid each other by the exchange of facts and ideas from experience, but rather groups of men of all professions who were to receive, adapt, and disseminate the knowledge of the progress accomplished in other countries. So the preface to the Laws and Regulations of the Massachusetts Society for Promoting Agriculture[1] reads: "One great object of this Society will be, to obtain and publish an account of the improvements of other countries, and to procure models of the machines in which they excel. It will attend to whatever relates to rural affairs, and especially to promote an increase of the products of our lands, ... To encourage the utmost attention to these objects, the Society will, from time to time, offer such premiums as their funds will admit. They consider agriculture in all its various branches and connexions as highly interesting to all mankind. The wealth and importance of the community, is so intimately connected with, and dependent on the extent and success of agriculture, that every one who is desirous of advancing the happiness, prosperity, and dignity of his country, its commerce, and convenient subsistence of individuals, will lend his aid to this most useful institution."[2] The appeal of the society organized in Philadelphia in 1785 is equally broad.

These appeals were answered in the spirit in which they were

references are continually made to the superior agriculture of Europe and to the necessity of adopting and adapting its methods. "As other countries receive the benefits of our labours, in the products supplied to them, ... it is fit that we should profit by their experience in the arts of cultivation . . . ." p. viii. This society acknowledged its indebtedness to prominent European agriculturists by electing them to honorary membership. Arthur Young, William Bakewell, and Count Castiglioni, of Milan, were so honored.

[1] Organized 1792.

[2] Published in Boston, 1793. Agric. Repository, Vol I., pp. iii–iv.

[3] Here we read: "THE PHILADELPHIA SOCIETY FOR PROMOTING AGRICULTURE, was formed . . . . , by some citizens, only a few of whom were actually engaged in husbandry, but who were convinced of its necessity; and of the assistance which such an association, properly attended to, would afford to the interests of agriculture. . . . Many citizens have a mistaken idea, that their not being *agriculturists*, disqualifies them from becoming useful members of our Society . . . . The interests of *Commerce*, *Arts*, and *Manufactures*, form, with *Agriculture*, an indissoluble union; to which citizens of every class and calling, have it amply in their power to contribute." Memoirs, Vol. I. pp. ii, iv (note).

issued. An examination of the early membership of these societies shows that they were composed of men in whose lives agriculture was only one of many interests, and often the least important of all. There were in the Massachusetts society men of legal education, who had become prominent in political life, such as Samuel Adams, James Sullivan, then attorney-general of the state and later governor, General Joseph Lincoln, then Collector of the port of Boston, Christopher Gore, John Lowell and Jonathan Mason, all lawyers and active in politics and government. Besides these there were merchants, such as Stephen Higginson, Charles Vaughan and Azor Orne. We find also representatives of the other two professions, ministers and doctors, who, blessed with an outlook on the affairs of the community beyond their immediate duties, turned their attention to improvements in agriculture.[1] The interest of such men as these in agriculture, although no doubt genuine, was nevertheless far different in nature and in intensity from that of the inland farmer who was toiling day in and day out on his 100 acres, endeavoring to make a living for himself and his family. The contrast in point of view which must have existed between the "literary" and the practical agriculturists is evident from such a statement as that of General Warren, in the American Museum. He gives his reasons for being interested in agriculture in the following words: "Agriculture has long been a favourite object with me. In a philosophic view, it is great and extensive; in a political view, it is important, and perhaps the only firm and stable foundation of greatness. As a profession, it strengthens the mind, without enervating the body. In morals, it tends to increase virtue, without introducing vice. In religion, it naturally inspires piety, devotion, and a dependence on providence, without a tincture of infidelity. It is a rational and agreeable amusement to a man of leisure, and a boundless source of contemplation and activity to the industrious."[2]

The influence of these societies on the progress of agriculture in this period, on the methods employed by the farmers in rural com-

[1] Such were the Rev. Manasseh Cutler and Cotton Tufts, the physician. The Philadelphia society included such famous persons as John Dickinson, the president of the state, Tench Coxe, merchant and publicist, and Hugh Brackenridge, lawyer and editor. It is interesting to note in this connection that the two most important treatises on agriculture published before 1800 in New England were the work of clergymen, Rev. Jared Eliot, of Killingworth, Connecticut, and Rev. Samuel Deane, of Portland, Maine. See Appendix C.

[2] Op. cit., II. 344.

munities, was so slight as to be practically negligible. They were "a voice crying in the wilderness," forerunners of improvements comparable to those which had already taken place abroad. But for reasons which we shall presently set forth, the time was not ripe for the acceptance of their doctrines and propaganda. Their principal service was in preparing the way for future progress.[1]

The Contemporary Criticisms were Deserved.

Reviewing for a moment the evidence presented in the foregoing paragraphs, we can see clearly that the criticisms of New England agriculture at the beginning of the nineteenth century were fully deserved. The tillage of the fields was but a superficial scratching of the surface soil with clumsy tools; very little care was taken to preserve or increase the fertility of the soil by crop rotation or even by the simple and obvious method of applying manures; because of the neglect of root crops, the fodder for live stock was insufficient; the lack of nourishment, coupled with imperfect shelter and inattention to the principles of selection in breeding, had caused a general degeneration in practically all kinds of domestic animals. The same lack of intelligent effort, seen in the neglect of the productivity of his land and stock, is evident in the farmer's management of his orchards and woodlands. In general, the system of agriculture was not only extensive but even in many respects predatory; the farmers had little stimulus to get anything beyond a living, and in getting that they had little regard for the effects which their system of husbandry might have on the prosperity of future proprietors of their land.

[1] There were perhaps a dozen of these societies organized, principally in cities on the eastern seaboard, before 1800. Among this number were those organized in Charleston, S. C., in 1784; in Philadelphia, in 1785; in New York, 1791; and in Boston, 1792. Besides these there were a few smaller societies such as the Western Society of Middlesex Husbandmen, 1794; the Kennebec Agricultural Society, 1800; and the New Haven County (Conn.) Agricultural Society, 1803. In the smaller societies the practical farmers seem to have formed a large, perhaps a predominant element, but the initiative and direction came from men whose interest in agriculture was but subsidiary to other interests. See Carver, Historical Account, p. 56; and Butterfield, K. L., Art. Farmers' Social Organizations, in Bailey's Cyclopedia of American Agriculture, IV. 290–291. The manuscript Proceedings of the New Haven society are preserved in the library of Yale University. The transactions of some of the larger societies, such as those in Philadelphia and Boston, were published, along with various contributed articles. These publications are more valuable for the light they shed on the state of scientific knowledge of agriculture than for information on the current practices of farmers.

But the Explanation Given was not Sufficient.

The reasons for the foregoing state of affairs generally given by contemporary and later writers on the subject may be grouped under three chief heads: (1) the ignorance of the farmers of what we now recognize as the fundamental principles of scientific agriculture; (2) the conservatism which bound them down to traditional methods; (3) the cheapness of land and the consequent high price of labor. All of these conditions undoubtedly existed and each contributed in its own way to prevent progress, yet none of them, it seems to me, would alone, or in combination with the others, have been able to prevent progress in agriculture if it had not been for the presence of another and more decisive condition, the lack of a market.

Inefficiency of Agriculture was not Due to Ignorance.

The typical inland farmer was undoubtedly ignorant of the best methods of tillage and of fertilization, and of the fact of increased productivity which the application of these methods would bring. But this was not a necessary or an inevitable state of affairs. The knowledge of the improvements which had been accomplished abroad was accessible in this country. Beginning with the publication of the first of the Reverend Jared Eliot's Essays on Field Husbandry in New England, in 1749,[1] an unwearying attempt had been made by men of education to bring to the attention of farmers in the Eastern states, and particularly in New England, the importance of changing their methods. The result had been the publication of a respectable body of literature on the subject, including at least sixteen works[2] of a general nature, in which the contrast between the methods employed at home and abroad were pointed out, the improvements introduced by Tull, Bakewell and Young were outlined and discussed in simple language, and suggestions were made for adapting their discoveries to the conditions prevailing here. Besides these there were published a considerably larger number of pamphlets, dealing with special branches of the agricultural industry, such as the use of gypsum as a fertilizer, the advantages of rotation of crops, the breeding of sheep and the management of bees. The agricultural societies were spreading similar information through their published reports, and such periodicals as The Old Farmer's Almanack

---

[1] These essays, six in all, appeared separately in the years 1749–1759, and were in 1760 published in collected form.

[2] About half of these were published before 1800. For a partial list of titles of the general and special works on agriculture published in this country before 1815, see Appendix C.

and the American Museum[1] were helping along the cause of education by repeated admonitions, "in season and out of season."

Little could have been expected in the way of results from this propaganda, if the farmers had not been fitted by nature or training to receive it. But it seems evident that the New England farmers were both intelligent and educated enough to see the advantages of the new husbandry and to apply its methods. It is universally recognized that the general level of education was at this time higher in New England than in any other part of the country. Common schools, at which attendance was compulsory, were found in every town[2] almost as soon as it was settled. The terms in these schools were, it is true, short, and the teachers often inefficient, but even if the bulk of the pupils never progressed beyond the rudiments, still the training was universal and furnished a valuable working equipment.[3] There is also evidence at hand that the farmers showed a disposition to utilize and improve their knowledge by reading. "Social libraries" were found even at this early date in many of the older towns and parishes,[4] and newspapers, both those which were published in the inland towns themselves and those from the commercial towns,[5] were read everywhere with avidity. So widespread

[1] The American Museum appeared monthly in the years 1787–1792. It was published in Philadelphia but seems to have had many readers and contributors in New England. The Old Farmer's Almanack was established by Isaiah Thomas in Worcester in 1793 and has appeared annually since that date.

[2] An exception should be made for certain towns in Rhode Island. In that state the law requiring the establishment and maintenance of such schools had been repealed a few years before 1810. See Morse, Gazetteer, 1810, art. R. I.

[3] No doubt the value of the education received in these schools has been overrated along with other features of "the good old days," especially in comparison with the training given to children in modern schools. Here we are concerned with its absolute rather than with its relative value. See Adams, C. F., Episodes, II. 781.

[4] In Pease and Niles' Gazetteer of Connecticut and Rhode Island the social library is almost as regularly mentioned in the descriptions of the various towns as are the saw-mills or the ministers and doctors.

[5] As early as 1790, there were 37 periodicals published in New England, of which three appeared semi-weekly, 32 weekly, and two monthly. U. S. Department of Commerce and Labor, Bureau of the Census. A Century of Population Growth. Washington. 1909. pp. 32–34. A few years later, according to Dwight, Travels, IV. 344–345, the total had grown to 55. Before 1800 newspapers had been established in such inland towns as Worcester, Pittsfield, Stockbridge, Greenfield, Northampton and Brookfield, in Massachusetts; in Litchfield, Windham and Danbury, in Connecticut; in Brattleboro and Rutland, in Vermont; and in Hanover, Keene, Concord, Amherst, Walpole, and Gilmanton, in New Hampshire. See U. S. Library of Congress. Check List of American Eighteenth Century Newspapers. Washington. 1912.

was this habit that not only did travelers comment upon it,[1] but the conservative Dwight was moved to remark: "The reading of newspapers in this country is undoubtedly excessive, as is also the number of such papers annually published."[2] The same author however, recognized clearly the advantages of education in general on the productive capacity of the community, setting them forth as follows: "A New Englander imbibes, from this education, an universal habit of combining the objects of thought, and comparing them in such a manner as to generalize his views with no small degree of that readiness and skill, which in many countries are considered as peculiar to a scientifical education. Hence he often discerns means of business and profit, which elsewhere are chiefly concealed from men of the same class. Hence, when prevented from pursuing one kind of business, or unfortunate in it, he easily, and in very many instances successfully, commences another. Hence he avails himself of occurrences, which are unregarded by most other men. . . . . Universally our people are, by this degree of education, fitted to make the best of their circumstances, both at home and abroad; to find subsistence where others would fail of it; to advance in their property, and their influence where others would stand still; and to extricate themselves from difficulties where others would despond."[3]

As an instance of the effects of this universal education in quickening intelligence, Dwight cites one of those "many original machines for abridging human labour, and improving its results," the stocking-loom. He might have cited the machine for cutting and heading nails and tacks,[4] the system of interchangeable parts in the manu-

---

[1] Foreigners traveling in this country remarked upon the wide circulation of newspapers. Lambert while on a journey from Boston to Walpole, in New Hampshire, noticed that the stage-coach driver distributed these papers along the route, remarking: "There is scarcely a poor owner of a miserable log hut, who lives on the border of a stage road, but has a newspaper left at his door." Travels, II. 498–499. Rochefoucauld had written somewhat earlier of Massachusetts: "Not a house is to be found in the most remote corners of the country, where a newspaper is not read; and there are few townships that do not possess little libraries formed and supported by subscription." Travels, II. 215.

[2] Travels, IV. 344, note.

[3] Ibid., IV. 348=349. For a detailed description and discussion of educational facilities provided in New England see Ibid., pp. 282–298.

[4] A patent for such a machine was issued to one Jesse Reed of Boston, 1807. See Bishop, History of American Manufactures, II. 125–126. A similar machine was invented by Jacob Perkins of Newburyport, Mass., about 1790. See Swank, J. M. The Manufacture of Iron in New England. In the New England States, I. 374.

facture of muskets, perfected by Eli Whitney in New Haven,[1] and improvements in a number of other lines of manufacture, such as the making of tin plate in Meriden, in Connecticut, and the manufacture of wooden clocks in Waterbury, all of which displayed the ingenuity of his countrymen along mechanical lines. Why was it that this spirit of progress and invention, this capacity to work out new ideas and to apply the ideas of others did not display itself in agriculture? Certainly there was a large field for improvement there. The answer is simple. The application of genius and energy along mechanical lines was profitable, because a market could be found for the improved and increased product; a market for increased agricultural produce was not at hand, therefore progress along that line was not remunerative.

Conservatism.

Conservatism has always been acknowledged as a characteristic quality of any agricultural population, especially in countries where the land is held in small tracts in fee simple and cultivated by the owners. New experiments are always made reluctantly; with limited resources the failure of a single crop may bring disaster. The New England farmers were undoubtedly conservative,[2] but it seems illogical to select this quality of their minds as a determining factor in the explanation of the lack of agricultural progress. For if conservatism had been so important it would have affected not only the inland farmers but also those of the coast regions. The latter had behind them the same ancestry and the same traditions, the conditions of land tenure were the same; but yet, as we have seen, they did not hesitate to make new ventures, to invest labor and capital in their farms, to modify their practices in any way that seemed to offer more profit.

Land was Cheap and Labor Dear—Washington's Explanation.

The third argument, that concerning the relative prices of land and labor, deserves more serious consideration. It is given most prominence by those writers who were intelligently seeking an economic explanation of the phenomena they observed. So Washington wrote: "An English farmer must entertain a contemptible opinion

---

[1] See Dwight, Statistical Account of New Haven, pp. 38–39.

[2] General Warren wrote: "Our farmers have all along followed the practice of their fathers, which might be adopted, at first, from necessity, and is pursued from want of spirit to adopt a better and more rational system by those who are convinced of the absurdity of it." American Museum, II. 346.

of our husbandry, or a horrid idea of our lands, when he shall be informed that not more than eight or ten bushels is the yield of an acre: but this low produce may be ascribed, ... to a cause which I do not find touched by either of the gentlemen whose letters are sent to you, namely that the aim of the farmers in this country (if they can be called farmers) is, not to make the most from the land, which is or has been cheap, but the most of the labour, which is dear: the consequence of which has been, much ground has been *scratched* over, and none cultivated or improved as it ought to have been; whereas a farmer in England, where land is dear and labour cheap, finds it his interest to improve and cultivate highly that he may reap large crops from a small quantity of land."[1]

Livingston wrote in much the same strain. Speaking of the disparagements cast upon the agriculture of this country by foreigners, he says: "To this we must add an erroneous idea, that most strangers entertain of the perfection of agriculture: they presume, that it consists in obtaining the greatest quantity of produce from a given quantity of land; and when they find that the arable yield of our fields is less than that of their native country, they at once pronounce us miserable farmers; not considering, that agriculture is good, or bad, in proportion to the return which it makes for the capital employed, and that the capital consists not of land only, but of stock, land, and labour. In countries in which a great population causes land to be dear, and labour cheap, the farmer expends much labour on little land, and renders that extremely productive, and the reverse where land is cheap, and labour dear. . . . . Considered in this view, we are much inclined to think, that the agriculture of the United States is at least equal to that of Europe; . . . ."[2]

The Effect of Cheap Land—The Frontier.

In an examination of the influence of the relative values of land and labor on agricultural methods and progress, it seems to me that

---

[1] This letter of Dec. 5, 1791, addressed to Arthur Young, is quoted by Blodget, Samuel, Junior. Economica: A Statistical Manual for the United States of America. Washington. 1806, p. 91. It is not, however, found in either Sparks' or Ford's editions of Washington's works. It was supposed to have accompanied a description of agriculture in the United States, which, in response to Young's request, Washington had compiled from queries addressed to prominent men in various states.

[2] American Agriculture, pp. 332–333. In a later passage, p. 341, the writer admits that such a system may be disastrous for the community, even if it be justified from the point of view of the individual's interest.

attention should be concentrated on the causal factor, the cheapness of land. The high price of labor may have affected the calculations and management of the farmers in the few favored regions, such as the towns in the neighborhood of Boston, but it is difficult to see how this condition could have had any significance for the farmers in inland towns. To farmers who never hired any labor, what difference could it make whether the price of labor was high or low? For the ordinary operations of farm life, directed only to supply a single family with the necessaries of life, the labor force of that family was sufficient. To spend any amount, however small, in hiring labor to raise a surplus of crops or live stock for which no market could be found would have been economic folly.

The cheapness of land, on the other hand, was a matter of vital importance. In a new country where land is cheap we naturally expect to find an extensive system of agriculture. When, however, a country, or a section of it, becomes fully settled, as New England was in 1810, an increase in population demands an increase in the supply of foodstuffs. Under an extensive or a predatory system of cultivation, a stage of diminishing returns is soon reached at which this increased supply can be obtained only at a more than proportional expense of labor and capital. Two courses are then open to the farmers. Either they must send the surplus of their population to new lands in another section of the country, or, if such lands are unavailable, they must if possible amend their methods, introduce improvements and so postpone the stage of diminishing returns. At any rate, an increased product must be forthcoming; either emigration will ensue or a more intensive system of cultivation must be adopted. Now it was the presence of large tracts of uncleared land, of as great if not of greater fertility than that which the farmers of inland towns were then cultivating, to be had almost for the asking, which persuaded them to choose the former of these alternatives.

Emigration.

Emigration began from the older towns before 1750, first to the as yet unsettled counties in the northern and western sections of Massachusetts, and after the Revolution to the states of northern New England.[1] Thus the annual surplus of population was drained off and the remainder managed to get a living without introducing new methods of agriculture. Tudor describes this process and its

[1] For a fuller consideration of the amount and direction of emigration in this period, see Appendix B, pp. 383 ff.

results as follows: "The spirit of emigration, acting with full force
on an enterprising people, easily induced them to go to new states
in pursuit of the real or delusive advantages that were held out to
them. This constant draining from our population, while it afforded
a hardy, vigorous race for the cultivation of new territories; may
have produced a greater increase to the ultimate good and power
of the nation, than would have happened if these emigrants had
remained stationary; still it occasioned some local disadvantages.
In the first place it prevented the inhabitants from thinking of any
improvement; if their farm was not sufficiently productive, the easy
remedy to a restless people was to sell it, collect their effects and go
five or fifteen hundred miles (the distance, greater or less, was not
thought of) in pursuit of a richer soil. It was not by the employment of greater skill, but by a change in location, that they sought
to improve their condition."[1]

*The Real Cause of Inefficient Agriculture was the Lack of a Market
for Farm Products.*

The ignorance and the conservatism of the farmers were undoubtedly to some extent hindrances to agricultural progress; cheap land
on the frontier discouraged intensive cultivation at home; but these
circumstances do not, either alone or in combination, furnish a sufficient explanation for the state of the industry which prevailed.
In the background lay a condition of much more significance, because
of its determining force upon all the others. I refer to the lack of a
market for agricultural products. Once given a market, neither
ignorance of the improved methods of agriculture nor the reluctance
to experiment along new lines, proceeding from a conservative disposition, nor the cheapness of land, inviting extensive cultivation,
could long have stood in the way of progress. If the farmers of
the inland towns had had an opportunity to exchange for the products
of the outside world their grain, meat and dairy products, they would
have seized upon every scrap of information regarding the means
by which their fields and live stock could be made more productive;
their adherence to traditional methods would have been weakened,
and they would have applied to the conduct of agriculture the same
adventurous and ingenious spirit which they displayed in the field
of mechanical invention and in that of commercial enterprise. Labor
might still have been expensive, yet they would have employed others
to work for them. The expense of labor was at this time a hin-

[1] Letters on the Eastern States, pp. 234–235.

drance to the growth of manufactures, also, but when the market was opened through the failure of European competition, during the period of the Embargoes and the War of 1812, manufacturers found it profitable to employ workers even at the high wages demanded.

In fact we have repeatedly noted in the preceding sections of this chapter that wherever a body of farmers were so situated as to be able to reach a market, whether in the commercial towns of the seacoast or in the West Indies, there these obstacles to progress had already, to some extent, been overcome. Dickinson recognized this fact when he wrote: "Our farmers prefer exerting their labor upon a large field, to employing the same on a small one. Deviating, however, from this rule, in the vicinity of populous towns, and on navigable waters, where the price of land enters more highly into the farming capital, they have paid more attention to husbandry, and increased their produce by additional expenditures of labor."[1] Had this author carried his analysis only one step farther and asked himself the question, "Why is the price of land higher in the vicinity of populous towns and on navigable waters?" the answer would have given him a much more fundamental reason for the improvements which he observed. It was the presence of a market, an opportunity to sell produce, which increased the competition for these lands, which made the farmer willing to pay highly for the opportunity of entering that market.

On the other hand, all other stimuli to agricultural improvement were futile as long as the market was lacking. We have seen that the campaign of education of the latter part of the eighteenth century was without results. It is difficult to see how a cheaper labor force could have produced any different results. The revolution in agriculture, as well as the breaking down of the self-sufficient village life, awaited the growth of a non-agricultural population. Between the years 1810 and 1860 such a population arose in the manufacturing cities and towns of New England, and the market thus created brought changes which opened up a new era to the farmers in the inland towns.

[1] Geographical and Statistical View, p. 8.

CHAPTER VI.

At the conclusion of the survey of economic conditions in southern New England in 1810 which occupied the first four chapters of this essay, we ventured the statement that the most important circumstance determining the life of the inhabitants of inland towns was the lack of a market. In the preceding chapter the assertion has been partially justified by an examination of the effect of this circumstance, this commercial isolation of the inland town, on the agricultural industry carried on by its inhabitants. It remains for this chapter to consider to what extent the peculiar characteristics of home and community life in these towns were also dependent on the same cause. The best place to look for the influence of a market, or the effects of a lack of it, is in the everyday life of the farmer himself. If our reasoning up to the present has been accurate, we should expect to find him unable to sell more than a trifling amount, if any, of the produce of his land, and consequently unable to purchase goods to any considerable extent from the outside world. He and his family must have constituted very nearly an economic microcosm, a self-sufficient household economy, supplying their wants almost entirely by their own labor, except for occasional neighborly coöperation, and relying hardly at all on the exchange of products or services with outside communities.

The Self-sufficiency of New England Farms.

The facts, as far as they can be learned, give ample support to this deduction. It would naturally be expected that, given the soil and climate of New England which lend themselves to the cultivation of a variety of food products, the farmer would be able to provision his family from his own land, but the extent of this self-sufficiency is somewhat surprising. Dwight tells us[1] that flesh and fish were the principal food of the inhabitants of New England. A more concrete description of their fare is that given by Felt: "For more than a century and a half (*i.e.*, up until almost 1800) the most

[1] Travels, IV. 341.

354

of them had pea and bean porridge, or broth, made of the liquor of boiled salt meat and pork, and mixed with meal, and sometimes hasty pudding and milk—both morning and evening."[1] Except for the salted cod which made a favorite Saturday dinner for families a considerable distance inland, the use of fish was probably confined to the seacoast regions and to towns along the rivers where fishing was regularly carried on,[2] as a by-industry of agriculture. Beef, pork, and mutton were all supplied from the farmer's own flocks and herds. He was often his own butcher, although at times he called upon some neighbor for this service. Owing to the lack of facilities for refrigeration most of the meat was dried, salted or pickled,[3] operations performed by the women of the household. They also supplied the table with butter and cheese, and tried out the lard used in cooking.

The common bread of the country people was made of a mixture of Indian corn meal and rye flour ("rye and Injun"), ground at the local grist-mill from the farmer's own grains. Wheat bread was in common use only in the seaports, whither the grain was brought[4] from the Southern and Middle states, and in the region west of the Connecticut River, where the soil was best suited to the cultivation of this grain.[5] Fruits and vegetables grew everywhere in as great a variety and abundance as the farmer could find time to plant and cultivate. The orchards were especially important for their supplies of cider, the favorite drink of the country population.

Not only these staples of diet, but even some of the condiments which made them palatable were supplied from the farm. The business of making sugar and syrup from the sap of maple trees was a regular department of the routine operations of inland farms.

[1] History of Ipswich, p. 30.

[2] Supra Chapter II.

[3] A somewhat irregular supply of fresh meat was obtained by the practice of slaughtering an animal in alternation with one's neighbors and distributing parts of the carcass to the several families. A quarter of beef or mutton, or a side of pork could be consumed by a single family before it spoiled, whereas a large part of the meat would have been wasted, if not preserved in some way, had it all remained in one household. This practice still obtains in country districts. It is one of the few surviving remnants of the various forms of coöperation which were necessary in those days.

[4] Supra p. 303, note 5.

[5] Warden, D. B. Statistical, Political and Historical Account of the United States of North America. 3 vols. Edinburgh. 1819. Vol. I., p. 329, estimates that corn and rye bread was eaten by four-fifths of the inhabitants of Massachusetts. See also Dwight, Travels, I. 340.

The season, as marked off in the annual editions of the Old Farmer's Almanack,[1] was from the end of February until the beginning of April, a period when other outdoor operations were at a standstill. The apparatus required was simple and inexpensive, consisting merely of wooden troughs and buckets and iron kettles. The farmer and his sons collected the sap and the women of the family attended to the process of boiling or "sugaring-off," as it was called. With an average product of five pounds of sugar from each maple tree[2] it was not difficult to obtain in this way the whole annual supply of a family. Although generally of a poorer quality than the cane sugar from the West Indies which was used in the coast towns, yet when sufficient care was taken, a fine-grained, clear product could be obtained.[3] Another substitute for the cane sugar was the honey obtained from the hives of bees which were considered an important adjunct of every well-managed farm.[4] Although a single hive would yield from 30 to 40 pounds of honey, besides five or six pounds of wax, yet this was a much less important product than the maple sugar, principally because of the amount of attention which the bees required in the early summer, when the farmer was most busy with other operations.[5]

The articles of diet which the farmers used and which they could not produce were salt, tea and coffee, molasses and rum. The first of these was, of course, absolutely necessary, and consequently it formed one of the most important articles in internal trade. Molasses was another substitute for sugar, and the rum which was distilled from it either in New England or in the West Indies, was a beverage rivaling cider in its popularity. It was a favorite tavern tipple and in some of the more accessible towns it was supplied to farm laborers in the hay-fields.[6] Tea and coffee seem to have been coming into general use throughout New England at this time. Dwight says:

[1] Kittredge, The Old Farmer and his Almanack, pp. 121–123.

[2] Coxe, View, pp. 681–682. Coxe believed thoroughly in the importance of the maple sugar industry and in the possibility of obtaining the whole domestic supply from this source. Dwight claims to have known a single tree to yield fourteen pounds of sugar in a season. Of the quality of the product he says: "I have seen the grain of this sugar as large and fine as that of the best Muscovado." Travels, I. pp. 15–16.

[3] Belknap, History of New Hampshire, III. 113–116, gives a detailed description of the process of making maple sugar as observed in New Hampshire.

[4] See Notes on Farming, p. 38.

[5] Mass. Agric. Soc. Papers, II., 1807, 40–41.

[6] See advertisement in the Windham (Conn.) Herald, June 3, 1806.

"Tea and coffee constitute a part of the breakfast and supper of every class, and of almost every individual."[1] Coxe, speaking of the whole country, said that teas were consumed freely by rich and poor, and adds that in 1790 they formed one-seventh of the total imports.[2] In Barnstable County, Massachusetts, where the fisher-farmers were able to purchase more from the outside than the inland folk, the plentiful consumption of this stimulant was thought to be the cause of the prevalence of nervous complaints.[3] The difficulty with which tea and coffee were obtained by the inland farmer is shown by the list of substitutes to which resort was occasionally had. For tea, raspberry and blackberry leaves were used and instead of coffee, parched rye and chestnuts, and even potatoes roasted and ground to a powder.[4]

Clothing—The Age of Homespun.

In the matter of clothing the farm was quite as self-sufficient as in diet. The Age of Homespun[5] is a title which has been very appropriately applied to this period, recognizing as it does the predominant importance of the domestic textile industries. All the evidence available tends toward the conclusion that the inhabitants of the rural towns, both men and women, were clothed in fabrics spun and woven in their own homes from the wool and flax grown on their own flocks and in their own fields. Statesmen such as Hamilton and Gallatin early recognized the extent of this branch of domestic industry. The former wrote in 1791: "Great quantities of coarse cloths, coatings, serges, and flannels, linsey woolseys, hosiery of

[1] Travels, IV. 342. Both of these beverages were, however, of recent introduction. Felt tells us that the colonists in Ipswich were unfamiliar with the proper method of brewing tea until about 1760. Coffee had been used somewhat, but only by the wealthier families, before the Revolution. History of Ipswich, p. 28.

[2] View of the U. S., p. 117.

[3] See Mass. Hist. Soc. Coll., I. 3: 13.

[4] See Earle, Home Life, pp. 158–159; and Kittredge, The Old Farmer and His Almanack, p. 185. These substitutes must have been nearly as unsatisfactory as the bark of the prickly ash tree, which Belknap says was used by the back-country people of New Hampshire instead of pepper. History of New Hampshire, III. 125.

[5] This is the title of an address delivered by the Rev. Horace Bushnell at the Centennial Celebration of Litchfield County, Conn., in 1851. It is contained in a volume of his collected works entitled Work and Play. New York. 1864. pp. 368–402. In his address the author says much that is thoughtful and significant concerning the effects of the self-sufficient family economy on the formation of individual character and on the social life of the village communities.

wool, cotton, and thread, coarse fustians, jeans, and muslins, checked and striped cotton and linen goods, bed ticks, coverlets and counter-panes, tow linens, coarse shirtings, sheetings, towelling and table linen, and various mixtures of woolen and cotton, and of cotton and flax, are made in the household way, and, in many instances, to an extent not only sufficient for the supply of the families in which they are made, but for sale, and even, in some cases, for exportation.[1] It is computed in some districts that two-thirds, three-fourths, and even four-fifths, of all the clothing of the inhabitants, are made by themselves."[2] Twenty years later Gallatin wrote: "But by far the greater part of the goods made of those materials (cotton, flax, and wool) are manufactured in private families, mostly for their own use, and partly for sale. They consist principally of coarse cloth, flannel, cotton stuffs and stripes of every description, linen, and mixtures of wool with flax or cotton. The information received from every State and from more than sixty different places, concurs in establishing the fact of an extraordinary increase, during the last two years, and in rendering it probable that about two-thirds of the clothing, including hosiery, and of the house and table linen, worn and used by the inhabitants of the United States, who do not reside in cities, is the product of family manufactures."[3]

More significant than these statements, however, because apply-ing specifically to New England, are those to be found in the gazet-teers of the time. Pease and Niles say of Connecticut: "The domes-tic manufactures in this State are extensive and important, and consist of woolen, linen, and cotton; but the former is by far the most important. With the exception of the cities, almost every family manufactures the substantial woolen fabrics, for their own consumption."[4] Of the same state Morse says: "The farmers in

---

[1] In Gallatin's Report on Manufactures (1810), the textile manufactures of families in New Hampshire are estimated to average from 100 to 600 yards in a year. Of their sale we read: "Considerable quantities of coarse flaxen cloth, worth from 15 to 20 cents a yard, thus manufactured in families, are sold to traders in the country villages or in towns, and sent for a market to the Southern States, on which a profit is made by the trader." In American State Papers, Finance, II. 435. We find occasional references to the purchase of homespun cloth by the country stores in the advertisements of such newspapers as the Windham (Conn.) Herald. There is not sufficient evidence of this sort, however, to lead to the conclusion that this manufacture of cloth for export by farmers' families was uniformly found in inland towns.

[2] Report on Manufactures, 1791. In American State Papers, Finance, I. 132.
[3] Report on Manufactures, 1810. In American State Papers, Finance, II. 427.
[4] Gazetteer, p. 17.

Connecticut, and their families, are mostly clothed in plain, decent, homespun cloth. Their linens and woolens, are manufactured in the family way; . . . ."[1] In the statistical descriptions of various towns we find such statements as this: "The people generally manufacture their woolen and linnen cloaths in their own families, using all of their wool and most of their flax."[2] If we could have examined the wardrobes of the men and women of the rural towns piece by piece, we should have found everything of household manufacture,[3] with the exception of the few bits of Sunday finery, hard earned and long-treasured, such as a beaver hat, shoe-buckles, or a fancy waistcoat, a silk gown and a few ribbons.

The best description of the dress of the country folk at the beginning of the last century, which I have been able to find, is that contained in a manuscript prepared by Governor Treadwell of Connecticut, in the year 1802 or 1803. The governor lived in Farmington, a town ten miles west of Hartford on the Farmington River. The conditions of dress and life which he describes are of the period 1760-1770. He remarks that between that time and 1800 a considerable change had taken place, owing to the increasing commerce between the town and the outside world, via Hartford and the Connecticut River. Such a change had, however, not yet taken place in towns less favorably situated, and for them the conditions described still obtained. In fact, the homespun garb prevailed in some districts for several decades after 1800. Rev. Horace Bushnell said in 1851 to the people of Litchfield County, Connecticut: "You have remembered the wheel and the loom. You have recalled the fact that our Litchfield County people, down to a period comparatively recent, have been a people clad in homespun fabrics—not wholly, or in all cases, but so generally that the exceptions may be fairly disregarded."[4]

Governor Treadwell wrote as follows: "Our ancestors here, of both sexes, have, till of late, clad themselves in simple apparel, suited to their moderate circumstances and agricultural state. The

[1] Gazetteer, 1810, art. Connecticut.

[2] Goodrich, Rev. Samuel. A Statistical Account of Ridgefield in the County of Fairfield (Conn). MS. in the library of the Connecticut Historical Society Hartford, Conn., p. 5. The date is uncertain. The manuscript was deposited in the library in 1800; internal evidence indicates that it was written a few years earlier.

[3] Women's hats were at times of household manufacture. See Gallatin, Report on Manufactures, p. 439. Also Earle, Home Life, pp. 259–261.

[4] Age of Homespun, p. 372.

men have been content with two suits of clothes, called the every-
day clothes, and the Sabbath-day clothes. The former were usually
of two sorts, those for labour, and those for common society. Those
for labour in the summer were a check homespun linen shirt, a pair
of plain tow-cloth trowsers, and a vest generally much worn, formerly with, but more modernly without sleeves; or simply a brown
tow-cloth frock and trowsers, and sometimes a pair of old shoes tied
with leather strings, and a felt hat, or an old beaver hat stiffened and
worn white with age. For the winter season they wore a check blue
and white woolen shirt, a pair of buck-skin breeches, a pair of white,
or if of the best kind, deep blue home-made woolen stockings, and a
pair of double soled cowhide shoes, blacked on the flesh side, tied with
leather strings; and, to secure the feet and legs against snow, a pair
of leggins, which, for the most part, were a pair of worn out stockings,
with the bottom and toe of the foot cut off, drawn over the stocking
and shoe, and tied fast to the heel and over the vamp of the shoe;
or if of the best kind, they were knit on purpose of white yarn, and
they answered for boots on all occasions; an old plain cloth vest
with sleeves, lined with a cloth called drugget: an old plain cloth
great coat, commonly brown, wrapped around the body, and tied
with a list or belt: or as a substitute for them, a buck-skin leather
waistcoat and a leather apron of tanned sheep-skin fastened round the
waist, and the top of it supported with a loop about the neck, and a
hat as above, or a woolen cap drawn over the ears.

"For ordinary society in summer, they were clad in a check linen
homespun shirt and trowsers, or linen breeches, white homespun
linen stockings, and cowhide single soled shoes, a vest with sleeves
usually of plain brown cloth, a handkerchief around the neck, a
check cap, and a hat in part worn.

"In winter they were clad as above described for summer except
that they assumed, if they had it, a better great coat, a neckcloth
and a hat that might be considered as second best. Their Sabbath-day
suit for winter, was like that last mentioned, except that their stockings were commonly deep blue, their leather breeches were clean and
of a buff colour, they added a straight-bodied plain coat and a white
holland cap, and sometimes a wig with a clean beaver hat. For the
summer it was a check holland shirt, brown linen breeches and stockings, single soled cow hide shoes with buckles, a plain cloth and sometimes a broadcloth and velvet vest, without sleeves: the shirt-sleeves
tied above the elbows with arm strings of ferreting of various colours,

a white holland cap or wig, and beaver hat: and on Thanksgiving days, and other high occasions, a white holland shirt and cambric neckcloth.

"The women have been, till within about thirty years past, clothed altogether in the same style, with a moderate allowance for the taste of sex. A minute description will not be attempted; a few particulars will characterize the whole. They wore home-made drugget, crape, plain cloth and camblet gowns in the winter, and the exterior of their under dress was a garment lined and quilted, extending from the waist to the feet. Their shoes were high-heeled, made of tanned calf-skin, and in some instances of cloth. In the summer they wore striped linen and calico gowns, cloth shoes and linen underdress: and every young lady when she had attained her stature, was furnished with a silk gown and skirt if her parents were able, or she could purchase them by dint of labour. Their head dress has always occupied a great share of their attention while in youth; it has always been varying, and every mode seems, in its day, the most becoming. Within the period just mentioned, the elderly women have worn check holland aprons to meeting on the Sabbath, and those of early life, and of the best fashion, were accustomed to wear them in their formal visits."[1]

The Organization of the Household Industries.

The production in the household of woolen and linen, and to some extent also cotton fabrics, not only clothing but also the necessary house furnishings, such as sheeting, toweling, blankets, and table linen, and even such coarse fabrics as rag carpets and grain bags, was a well-organized industry. The various successive stages in the conversion of the raw materials into the finished product were regularly assigned to members of the family according to their strength and skill. Thus the men sheared and washed the wool, and performed most of the laborious processes of breaking, swingling and hackling the flax to prepare the fiber for spinning. The carding of the wool, corresponding in a way to these processes, was for years the task assigned to the older members of the family whose strength and eyesight would have been unequal to more onerous and careful work. About the year 1800, however, the household was relieved of this task by the introduction of the water-power carding machines, which, as we have seen, spread so rapidly that they were to be found in almost every village in 1810.[2] The younger women of the family

[1] Printed in Noah Porter's Historical Discourse. Appendix, Note S, pp. 82–83.
[2] Supra p. 260.

spun the fibers thus prepared into yarn and thread on the large and small wheels then found in every farmhouse. Bleaching and dyeing were also a part of the multifarious activities of these women. In the latter process almost all the materials used, such as pokeberries, madder, goldenrod, the bark of the hickory, butternut and sassafras trees, and various flowers, could be found in the woods and fields. For producing the deep blue which was so popular, indigo must be imported, and this was one of the few standard commodities sold at the stores and by itinerant peddlers.

Weaving, the next stage in the production of homespun cloth, was not so uniformly performed in every household. Looms were, however, to be found in every house of considerable size, and many houses had a room, or an ell, especially devoted to these ponderous and noisy machines. Gallatin wrote in 1810: "Every farmer's house is provided with one or more wheels, according to the number of females. Every second house, at least has a loom for weaving linen, cotton, and coarse woolen cloths, which is almost wholly done by women."[1] It is probable that a considerable share of this work was taken over by men, some of whom may have carried it on as a regular trade.[2] There were often many smaller looms in the house

---

[1] Report on Manufactures. 1810. p. 435. The note from which this quotation is taken refers to household manufactures in New Hampshire. It is interesting to compare in this regard the figures given by a writer in the Massachusetts Historical Society's Collections, II. 7: 70, for Hillsborough County, New Hampshire. He found 5,490 looms, in a population of 49,282 (about 9,000 families) in 1810. According to Coxe, Digest of Manufactures, 1812, p. 667, in the back-country of Pennsylvania there was in one county, McKean, only one loom among a population of 142 persons. In three other counties the proportion was one to every 20 or 30 of population. The spinning wheels were much more numerous, averaging about one to a family.

[2] Miss Earle says, Home Life, pp. 212–213: "Every farmer's daughter knew how to weave as well as to spin, yet it was not recognized as wholly woman's work as was spinning; for there was a trade of hand-weaving for men, to which they were apprenticed. Every town had professional weavers. They were a universally respected class, and became the ancestors of many of the wealthiest and most influential citizens today. They took in yarn and thread to weave on their looms at their own homes at so much a yard; wove their own yarn into stuffs to sell; had apprentices to their trade; and also went out working by the day at their neighbors' houses, sometimes carrying their looms many miles with them." Miss Earle cites no authorities; the lists of tradesmen given in the statistical accounts of various towns in Connecticut make no mention of weavers, and the only confirmation I have been able to find, of her statement is an entry in the account book of Rev. Medad Rogers of New Fairfield, Conn., of money paid out for weaving. See infra, pp. 366-367.

on which the women made garters, points, glove-ties, hair-laces, stay-laces, shoe-strings, hat-bands, belts and breeches-suspenders, often called "galluses."[1] The production of these odds and ends of apparel shows in a striking manner the extent to which the household was self-sufficient in its supply of clothing. Knitting was an important branch of the domestic textile industry, producing the hosiery, mittens, shawls, comforters, etc., for all the family. It must be remembered that the foregoing discussion applies only to the conditions prevailing in inland towns. In the seaports and larger river towns, the inhabitants had long used clothing and household furniture of foreign manufacture.

The Building and Furnishing of Farmhouses.

In the furnishings of their homes, the inland farmers relied to a very limited extent on exchange with the world outside their immediate vicinity, and in fact supplied their wants, as in the matter of food and clothing, largely by the exertions of their own families. In the construction of their houses, those story-and-a-half structures with long sloping roofs which one may still occasionally see in the more isolated country regions, they utilized the timber growing in the vicinity, often on their own land, and employed as workmen those of their neighbors who carried on the carpenter's trade as a by-industry of farming.[2] Only a small amount of hardware was used and most of this, such as bolts and hinges, was made by the local blacksmith. The nails, which were used much more sparingly than now, were often made by the farmers themselves from nail rods purchased either from the local store or from a nearby slitting-mill.[3] Glass, which had

---

[1] Earle, Op. cit., p. 225. A detailed description of the technical processes of hand-weaving as carried on in those days is contained in Chapter X of that work, pp. 212–251. Other chapters which have been consulted are Chapters VIII and IX, pp. 167–211, describing the cultivation and preparation of the flax and woolen fibers.

[2] Supra p. 262 ff. The task of raising the heavy beams which constituted the frame of the structure into position was accomplished by the united efforts of a large number of neighbors. This is another example of the coöperation of inland farmers for the accomplishment of a task now undertaken by specialized workmen, and, like the husking-bee, was utilized as an occasion for social intercourse and amusement.

[3] Supra p. 270. Coxe says: "Nailmaking is frequently a household business in New England, a small anvil being found no inconvenience in the corner of a farmer's chimney." View of the United States, p. 269. In another place he estimates the quantity of nails used by an average household in building and repairing at ten pounds per annum. Ibid. p. 144.

probably in all except the newest settlements replaced the wooden shutters and oiled paper of earlier times, was practically the only material brought from any distance. The furniture, such as bed-steads, chairs, settles, and tables, could easily be produced by the local cabinet-maker, or even by a skilful carpenter. Besides making the homespun sheets and blankets, quilts and comforters, the women of the family made mattresses and pillows stuffed with the feathers of home-raised geese.[1] An inventory of table-ware and kitchen utensils brings to light only a few "boughten" articles and these were carefully treasured and handed down from parents to children. Wood was the material most used, in fact wherever possible; of it were made trenchers, drinking-cups and tankards, and even spoons. Pewter was also used for these articles to some extent; but china, porcelain, glass or silverware were rarely seen. In the kitchen, wooden and earthenware vessels predominated, pots of iron, brass or copper being comparatively rare.[2]

In his Statistical Account of Middlesex County (Conn.), Field states that not only clothing and furniture but also agricultural implements were, at the beginning of the nineteenth century, made by the farmers for themselves.[3] Wood was here again the principal material employed. The tools used by a farmer in Concord, New Hampshire, are thus described: "His plows were mainly of wood, the soles and coulters only being of iron, though the mould-boards were usually plated with sheets of that metal.

"The village blacksmith made his nails, his axes, his chains, as also his clumsy pitchforks, and flat-tined manure forks. . . . His

---

[1] Woman's work, it would seem, was truly endless at this time. Besides the tasks already enumerated, and such by-industries as the making of soap and candles, they often had the care of poultry or bees, milked cows and did light outdoor work, such as weeding gardens and gathering fruit and vegetables. Combined with the bearing and rearing of large families of children, these unremitting labors shortened the duration of life of the sex very considerably. In frontier settlements extreme illustrations of this fact, were found, such as that cited by Kendall, Travels, III. 130. Near Bath, Maine, he saw a burying-ground in which were the graves of ten married women, eight of whom had died between the ages of twenty-two and thirty years. The "consumption" to which he attributes their early deaths, was, if it existed, no doubt brought on by overwork.

[2] See Earle, Home Life, Chs. III. and IV. Bishop, American Manufactures, I. 488, remarks upon the scarcity of iron utensils at this time. Iron pots, not generally more than one or two, were considered sufficiently valuable to be included in the inventories of estates.

[3] Op. cit., p. 17.

carts and sleds were generally constructed on the farm and ironed by the blacksmith, the wheels of the former having felloes three inches wide, tired with short strips of flat iron. . . . His shovels were mainly of wood, having blades pointed with iron. His harrows, made often of a forked tree, had teeth sometimes of wood and sometimes of iron."[1]

The Versatility and Ingenuity of Yankee Farmers.

Besides these standard by-industries of the farmer, there were a diversity of other tasks to which he applied himself more or less regularly according to his especial "bent" and opportunities. On the seacoast, as we have seen, he was frequently a sailor or a fisherman for part of the year.[2] In inland towns he often plied some trade or other and was classed as an artisan as well as a farmer. Every farmer did a multitude of odd jobs for himself, such as repairing old buildings and building new, laying walls and stoning up wells, butchering pigs and cattle, making axe-handles and brooms, splitting staves and shingles, tanning leather and cobbling shoes. Occasionally he performed some of these tasks for a neighbor, who either had not the requisite skill or was too busy with strictly agricultural operations. Such service was probably more often repaid in kind than in currency. In this way the Yankee farmer acquired a reputation for ingenuity and a moderate ability in a variety of occupations, which has now become proverbial.[3] His ability as a Jack-of-all-trades was not due to any exceptional endowment of versatility. It was distinctly a product of the economic environment and of the persistent endeavors

[1] Walker, J. B. The Farm of the First Minister. Reprinted from Report of New Hampshire State Board of Agriculture, 1894. Concord, N. H., 1895, p. 18. The importance of wood in the economy of the inland farmer needs no emphasis. It was early recognized by Belknap who devotes a chapter, Ch.VIII., in the third volume of his History of New Hampshire, to an enumeration of the varieties of trees native in that state and discusses the peculiar uses of each.

[2] Chastellux says: "The seaman when on shore immediately applies himself to some handicraft occupation, or to husbandry, and is always ready at a moment's notice to accompany the captain his neighbor, who is likewise frequently a mechanic, to the fisheries." Travels, II. 250.

[3] This quality of ingenuity was recognized by Chancellor Livingston. He says of the farmer of the Northern states: "He can mend his plough, erect his walls, thrash his corn, handle his axe, his hoe, his sithe, his saw, break a colt, or drive a team, with equal address; being habituated from early life to rely on himself he acquires a skill in every branch of his profession, which is unknown in countries where labor is more subdivided." American Agriculture, p. 338.

of the New England farmer to adapt himself thereto.[1] The most significant because the most far-reaching feature of that environment was the lack of a market. The problem that confronted the farmer was to get a living for himself and his family, and to get as good a living as he could with the least expenditure of labor. If he had been able to devote all his attention to raising some particular product, with the proceeds of whose sale he could have purchased the services of specialized artisans and goods from abroad, he undoubtedly would have preferred to do so. It would have tremendously increased his efficiency in production, and would have lightened the labors of all the members of his family. But the lack of a market was an insuperable obstacle to specialization and consequently the family group was forced to rely upon itself and upon irregular exchange with other neighboring groups for the necessaries of existence, and to do without, in large measure, the comforts and luxuries.

Commodities Bought and Sold by a Minister-Farmer.

There is not sufficient evidence to warrant even an approximate numerical estimate of the amount of produce which the farmer did actually sell and of the commodities which he received in exchange. Occasionally, however, we come across an account book kept by an inhabitant of one of these inland towns, a farmer, a blacksmith, or a minister, which furnishes a concrete illustration of the small amount of buying and selling which took place. Such an account book is that of the Rev. Medad Rogers, the minister of New Fairfield, Connecticut, a small town on the western boundary of the state.[2] He had

---

[1] It may be objected that the tendency to invent is an instinctive activity; that there is, psychologically speaking, an "impulse to contrivance." If this is true, inventive ingenuity must be a general human endowment, not confined to any particular nation or race. But the degree of the manifestation of this "impulse," of its successful realization, its embodiment in practical appliances among any particular people at a given period in their history, must, it seems to me, be largely dependent on the conditions of their economic environment. In the inland towns of New England there was a far greater necessity for the development of this "impulse" than in other less self-sufficient communities. Where, on the small farm, a single family had to devise means to produce the most varied articles for its own consumption, there the opportunities for the application of inventiveness and ingenuity were most numerous, and the advantages to be gained from the use of such talents were most apparent. A consideration of economic and psychological aspects of inventiveness may be found in Professor Taussig's "Inventors and Moneymakers." New York. 1915. Chapter I.

[2] The population was 742 in 1810. The nearest outlet to a market was the Hudson River, from 20 to 25 miles distant.

the use of a farm of 100 acres and in addition a salary of $100, part of which was, as the accounts show, paid in kind. The accounts extend from 1784 to 1822, but the years in which they were most carefully kept are 1792 and 1793. In the one year and nine months from February 14, 1792, to November 13, 1793, his total purchases amounted to £23, 10 shillings and 11 pence. The items are as follows:

3 lbs. brown sugar	1 pair wool cards
10 lbs. iron	1 barlow penknife
1 iron pot	1 bbl. linseed oil and paints
1 iron skillet	1 set pencilled tea dishes and saucers
2 earthern basons	1 skein holland thread
2 chamber pots	½ bus. salt
1 earthern jug	2 lbs. ginger
1 small cream pot	1 lb. alum
3 milk pans	1 gal. um
1¼ yards satinet	1 gal. molasses
¾ yard everlasting[1]	7 smoking pipes
5 yards coating	1 yard tobacco

The entries of goods purchased in other years show the same predominance of necessary commodities which could not be produced on the farm. Chief among these were iron, of which in one year he bought 81 pounds besides a bundle of nail rods, and salt, with occasional purchases of molasses and rum. Other entries show purchases of 50 bricks, a pork barrel, six cider barrels, a broadcloth coat and a pair of shoes. The coat and the pencilled tea dishes were refinements of life which probably were considered necessary to the minister's social position and set him apart from the bulk of his parishioners.

The entries of sales are far less numerous. The chief items are dairy products. A rather astonishing sale of 451 pounds of cheese is among them. It went to the local storekeeper and was to be paid for half in cash and half in merchandise. All the other sales were small, such as two and one-half yards of tow cloth, seven pounds of flax, three pounds of butter, a hind quarter of beef and a barrel of cider.[2]

[1] A sort of cloth.

[2] The account book of the Rev. Mr. Rogers is preserved in the library of the New Haven County Historical Society, New Haven, Conn. A small pamphlet entitled Sundry Prices taken from Ye Account Book of Thomas Hazard, published at the Washington County (Rhode Island) Agricultural Fair Grounds, 1892, contains information of the same sort but for a somewhat earlier date. Hazard was a farmer of South Kingston, Rhode Island.

The Result of Self-sufficient Economy was a Low Standard of Living.

The effect of this self-sufficiency in family and in village life was a low degree of efficiency in the production of wealth in both these economic units. The lack of a market made specialization impossible, there was practically no well defined division of labor except that existing between the sexes. Hence the gains from the adaptation of individual talents to especial tasks, and from the acquisition of skill through continuous repetition of identical movements or processes were almost entirely absent. The farmer who must also be his own tool-maker, carpenter, wheelwright, mason and general handy man could not hope to acquire any great efficiency in agriculture. He had no time to devote to careful experiments in the culture of crops or the breeding of stock, or even to read the books in which the results of scientific investigation were even then recorded. On the other hand, the mason, carpenter, doctor or lawyer who had to interrupt the pursuit of his especial avocation in order to procure food and clothing for himself and his family by means of agriculture, could not hope to develop any great degree of efficiency as an artisan or as a professional man. The result was that the bulk of the population of New England was at this time on what we should now call a low standard of living, and even this standard was supported only by arduous and unremitting toil. One large-minded observer has said: "No mode of life was ever more expensive; it was life at the expense of labor too stringent to allow the highest culture and the most proper enjoyment. Even the dress of it was more expensive than we shall ever see again."[1] The raw materials for food, clothing and shelter were at hand in abundance, but in working up these materials into consumable commodities, the people of those days were at a very great disadvantage. Only when we compare the clumsy and ineffective apparatus with which they worked, such as the old-fashioned Dutch oven and the open fireplace, the spinning wheel and the handloom, with the modern cooking appliances and the power-driven spinning frames and looms, can we appreciate to some extent how "expensive" their life really was.

The Contrary Opinion Held by Travelers.

How, then, can we explain the general impression of comfort and ease in getting a living which seems to have been made upon contemporary observers? Numerous passages might be cited from the travelers who passed through New England from the close of the

---

[1] Bushnell, Horace. The Age of Homespun, p. 393.

Revolution up to 1810, praising the beauty and ease of the life of the rural population. A quotation from Dwight is typical. In a chapter on the Mode of Living of New Englanders, he says: "The means of comfortable living are in New England so abundant, and so easily obtained as to be within the reach of every man who has health, industry, common honesty, and common sense."[1] In another passage he uses such phrases as "comfortable subsistence," "universally easy circumstances," and "universal prosperity,"[2] in describing the life observed in his travels. Surely such expressions do not describe an especially arduous existence; far more do they remind us of the descriptions of that land flowing with milk and honey, the Promised Land of the ancient Hebrews. The apparent lack of agreement between such opinions and the conditions which we have described in this chapter may be explained by a number of considerations. In the first place, we must remember that the standards of measurement used by the writers of that time were not those of today. When they said that living in New England at that time was easy or comfortable, they did not mean absolutely so, but in comparison with conditions of life in some other country, or in New England at some former time. The conditions with which they were most familiar and which they undoubtedly used as a standard of comparison were those of frontier life in this country and of the common people of Europe in the eighteenth century.[3] Judged by either of these standards, life was easy and comfortable; judged by our standards, however, it was far different.

Then, again, we must take into account the fondness of all literary travelers, and President Dwight was no exception, for sweeping generalizations and large, well-sounding, mouth-filling phrases. For the economic historian a few bits of specific information are worth far more as evidence and should be given credence when they are in conflict with the former. Considerable of this specific evidence has been given in previous sections of this chapter.[4] Even if, however,

---

[1] Travels, IV. 341.

[2] Ibid., I. xv.

[3] As a matter of fact, we find these comparisons specifically made. See Dwight, Travels, II. 254, and American Husbandry, I. 70.

[4] See supra pp. 355–365. Such a seemingly unimportant point as the use or lack of shoes and stockings by country people has significance. There is abundant evidence that they did not feel they could afford these articles except as protection against the cold and for especial occasions, such as the Sunday religious services. See Wansey, Journal, p. 71; Harriott, Struggles through Life, II. 54; Larned, History of Windham, II. 388–389; New Hampshire Historical Society Collections. 10 vols. 1824–1893. Vol. V. (1837), pp. 226–227.

their generalizations were carefully drawn from all the evidence presented, we must inquire whether the conditions observed were typical of those prevailing over New England as a whole, or whether the observations were limited to some particularly favored regions. As a matter of fact, we know that but very few of the travelers through New England left the beaten track of the stage coach routes from New York to Boston. They came up to New Haven along the shores of the Sound. There they had a choice of routes; they either continued along the shore to Newport and Providence, and thence across Bristol, Plymouth or Suffolk Counties to Boston, or branching off to the northeast to Hartford and then following the Connecticut Valley up to Springfield, they turned due east and reached Boston by way of Worcester. Except for the stretch between Springfield and Worcester, both of these routes passed through towns which were favored by exceptional opportunities for trade and often, as, for instance, the towns in the Connecticut Valley, by especially fertile soil as well. It is no wonder that travelers' conclusions, based on this sort of selected evidence, were so favorable.

Wealth was Equally Distributed.

Perhaps another explanation of the optimistic strain, so habitual in travelers' descriptions of economic conditions prevailing in New England at this time, is that they mistook equality in the distribution of wealth for ease in production. That the two ideas were closely connected in their minds is evident. Lambert, for instance, says of the inhabitants of the central part of Connecticut: "The generality of the people live in easy independent circumstances; and upon that footing of equality which is best calculated to promote virtue and happiness among society."[1] Of the inhabitants of Hampshire County, Massachusetts, Dwight says: "They are also, as a body, industrious and thriving, and possess that middle state of property, which so long, and so often, has been termed golden; . . . . Few are poor, and few are rich."[2] In another place the same author remarks: "Great wealth, that is, what Europeans consider as great wealth, is not often found in these countries. But poverty is almost unknown."[3]

[1] Travels, II. 304.
[2] Travels, II. 254.
[3] Ibid. I. xv.

Agriculture was not a Means of Making Money.

Equality in distribution would, under the circumstances, naturally be expected. The lack of a market meant production by each family or village unit simply for its own consumption. "The house was a factory on the farm, the farm a grower and producer for the house."[1] Except in especially favored regions, agriculture was not a commercial business; there was practically nothing raised for sale. Hence the opportunities for business profits, for the accumulation and investment of capital, all of which are necessary steps in the development of inequalities in wealth, were lacking.

The conditions of land tenure and the uniformity in the size of the farms are both proofs of this contention. It is well known that almost every farmer owned his own land, tenancy being found in only a few localities.[2] The farms varied in size from 80–100 to 250–300 acres, few having less than 100 acres and few more than 200.[3] Occasionally we find instances of families in the older inland towns distinguished from their neighbors by the possession of considerable estates in land,[4] enabling them to have more of the refinements and comforts of life and even some of its luxuries. Such instances, however, were exceptions to the general rule of plainness and frugality.

---

[1] Bushnell, The Age of Homespun, p. 392.

[2] Dwight found some tenancy on the Connecticut coast, east of New London. In Stonington, for instance, he found about half of the farms cultivated by tenants, who were, however, in that position only until they could obtain enough capital to purchase land for themselves. Travels, III. 16. See also Tudor, Letters from the Eastern States, p. 406.

The practice of holding land in common, at least pasture lands, which was often introduced at the settlement of a new town, seems to have died out in most localities before the Revolution. In Ridgefield, for instance, the common lands were divided in 1760. Goodrich, Statistical Account, p. 9. See also Doyle, J. A., English Colonies in America. 5 vols. New York. 1882–1907. Vol. V. p. 16. The practice seems to have survived longest, in the Island of Nantucket and in Plymouth and Barnstable Counties in Massachusetts. See Kendall, Travels, II. 208–210; also Adams, H. B., The Germanic Origin of New England Towns, Ch. II.; and Village Communities of Cape Anne and Salem, Chs. IX. and X.; both in Vol. I. of Johns Hopkins University Studies in History and Political Science.

[3] For a fuller discussion of this point and authorities see supra pp. 321–322.

[4] The author of American Husbandry writes, Vol. I. p. 62, as if the English system of cultivation by tenant farmers of land of large proprietors was not an uncommon thing in southern New England before the Revolution. Such a system may have prevailed occasionally in regions of active internal trade (as in Windham County, Conn., see Larned, History of Windham County, II. 270, and Kendall, Travels, I. 315), but there is no evidence that it existed throughout isolated rural communities.

Land was Cheap, Hence no Class of Wage-Earners.

And yet the acquisition of a moderate amount of land was not a matter of any great difficulty. Tudor writes: "Every industrious man may look forward with certainty to becoming proprietor in fee simple of a small farm."[1] This ease with which land could be acquired was one of the principal causes of the prevailing equality in the distribution of wealth, and in fact, with the lack of a market, was a factor determining the whole character of the economic life of the population of New England at this time. In the first place, it brought about that phenomenon of high wages which was so often commented upon by travelers and other observers, native and foreign.[2] It was naturally hard to persuade a young man to work for day-wages when he could so easily establish himself as an independent farmer. This fact, together with the lack of a market, effectually prevented the rise of a body of agricultural laborers. Even in regions where a market was accessible it was difficult, at what were then considered extravagant wages, to obtain a labor force for commercial farming.[3] In other districts there was little demand for such labor. The self-sufficient farm furnished its own labor force, the farmer and his sons being in most cases quite well able to raise the crops and to care for the live stock which provided food and clothing for the family.[4] It would indeed have been poor economy to hire laborers to raise a surplus which could not be sold. Exceptional tasks were accomplished by the voluntary coöperation of neighbors. Occasionally a farmer's son would hire out for a few years to a neighbor, but such service was always looked upon as temporary, as merely a means of accumulating sufficient capital to establish the young man as an independent farmer. And just as among the independent artisans in the country towns there was no regularly defined, per-

[1] Letters on the Eastern States, p. 405.

[2] These observations were in many cases concerned with the difficulty or impossibility of establishing manufactures in the colonies or, later, in the states. See Franklin, Benjamin. Canadian Pamphlet, in Works, Sparks edition, IV. 19, 40–41. Also American Husbandry, II. 257–267.

[3] Harriott, Struggles through Life, II. 193–194, tells of his unsuccessful efforts to get laborers to work on a farm on Long Island.

[4] Livingston, American Agriculture, p. 338, says: "Most of our farmers cultivate their farms with their own hands, aided by their sons when of proper age to be serviceable. Women labor in the harvest, and in haying, and in planting corn, before they are mothers, but seldom afterwards." See also Dickinson, Geographical and Statistical View, p. 8.

manent body of hired workmen, so also there was no class of agricultural laborers.[1]

Paupers—Cost of Poor Relief—Causes of Poverty.

These facts, showing the wide distribution of the ownership of land, and the resulting lack of a permanent labor class, lend support to the general statements of contemporary writers concerning the equality in the distribution of wealth. They would seem, also, to lead naturally to the inference that there could have been little if any extreme poverty and little need for poor relief in these inland towns. Such an inference would be, however, not strictly in accord with the facts. Poverty did exist and the sums appropriated each year by the towns for the support of the paupers were large as compared with the other items in their budgets.[2] This poverty, however,

[1] Tudor says of "the hired people," Letters on the Eastern States, p. 405: "These latter were seldom born, and seldom died, servants; they served for a time, till their wages would enable them to begin clearing land for a farm." Dwight, also, has a significant paragraph on the character of the labor force in New England. He says: "We have in New England no such class of men as on the eastern side of the Atlantic are denominated peasantry. The number of those, who are mere labourers, is almost nothing, except in a few populous towns; and almost all these are collected from the shiftless, the idle, and the vicious. A great part of them are foreigners. Here every apprentice originally intends to establish, and with scarcely an exception actually establishes himself in business. Every seaman designs to become, and a great proportion of them really become, masters and mates of vessels; and every young man hired to work upon a farm, aims steadily to acquire a farm for himself, and hardly one fails of the acquisition." Travels, IV. 335.

[2] In the six towns of Middlesex County, Conn., the expense of poor relief varied from $400 to $1,700 in 1814, amounting on the average to a per capita tax of $0.366 (Field, Statistical Account of Middlesex County, p. 23); in Litchfield, Conn., there were 38 paupers in a population of 4,500, whose annual support cost $1,500 in 1811. (Morris, Statistical Account of Litchfield, p. 107.) The figures quoted by Adams, Episodes, II, 729, 912–913, for Quincy, Mass., seem quite exceptional. Here the expense of the poor increased from $1,000 in 1812 to $1,665 in 1813, being equal at the later date to the combined appropriations for the church and the schools. During the six years 1808–1813 the total amount of taxes raised in this town was $18,200 and of this over one-third went for poor relief. The population of this town was 1,300 in 1810. In the town of Kingston, in the same county (population 1,300 in 1810), the expense of poor relief averaged only $600 at this date. Mass. Hist. Soc. Coll., II. 3: 215.

In interpreting these figures allowance must be made for the expensive practice of farming out the town poor, which regularly prevailed. Only in the largest towns, such as New Haven and Middletown in Connecticut, had almshouses been erected. The best contemporary description of the various methods of poor relief employed is found in Field, Op. cit., pp. 22–24.

was of a different sort from that to which we are accustomed nowadays. It was not primarily, nor to as great a degree as at present, due to economic pressure, or to maladjustments in the industrial system. It was comparatively easy for any able-bodied person of energetic disposition and temperate habits to earn a tolerable subsistence. The paupers of that time included principally that class of persons whom we now class as unemployable; the mentally or physically incapable, the insane and the feeble-minded, the cripples, the orphans and the aged. There were no insane asylums, orphanages, homes for incurables or for old persons; consequently these unfortunates, if no relatives were present who were able or willing to support them, fell on the town for support. And besides these there were those who had become enslaved to the current vice of drunkenness.[1]

The Vice of Intemperance—Its Causes.

"The intemperance of the colonial period," says Charles Francis Adams, "is a thing now difficult to realize; and it seems to have pervaded all classes from the clergy to the pauper."[2] We have already remarked the large consumption of cider in the farmers' families and have commented upon the importance of the retail sale of stronger liquors in the business of the country stores and taverns. Every important occasion in home or church life, every rural festivity was utilized as an opportunity for generous indulgence in intoxicants. Neither the haying-season in early summer, nor the hog-killing season at the end of autumn could be successfully managed without the aid of liberal potations of "black-strap" and "stone-wall." Husking bees, house-raisings, training days, and even christenings, burials and ordinations were often disgraced by the drunkenness of participants.[3]

---

[1] The Rev. Mr. Goodrich wrote of the town of Ridgefield: "The number of poor who receive aid from the town do not excede 10 or 12 of which number 2 or 3 receive their whole support. . . . we have no poor that are chargeable but what become so by bodily imbecility." Statistical Account, p. 17. On this point Tudor wrote: "There are few persons here, who can suffer absolute distress from poverty. That which arises among the wealthier classes, from great reverses, I am not considering; but an uncertainty about the common means of subsistence can never happen in the country, except to the miserable drunkard, or the unfortunate victim of some bodily or mental infirmity, who of course are supported by the public when destitute of friends; the labouring man, with good health and good habits, may always obtain the comforts of life, and increase his savings." Letters on the Eastern States, p. 407.

[2] Episodes, II. 785.

[3] See Adams, Episodes, II. pp. 783–794. The annual numbers of the Old Farmer's Almanack are full of admonitions against drunkenness. See also Harriott, Struggles through Life, II. 205–206.

The craving for stimulants with its disastrous results on the fortunes of individuals and on the general moral tone of the community proceeded partly from the coarse and unvaried diet of the farming population, and probably to a larger extent, from a desire to relieve at least temporarily the dreary monotony of village life. There are always two opposing views current among the older generation concerning the relative virtues of their early days as compared with the conditions which they see about them in their declining years. Some look back to a sort of Golden Age and view all the features of the past through rose-colored spectacles. Others with a more optimistic frame of mind are quite willing to admit that the passage of the years has brought improvement along many lines and do not hesitate to glory in the progress that has been achieved under their eyes during a long life. One of the best sources of information concerning the character of social life in the inland towns a century ago are the memorial discourses delivered upon the centennial and other anniversary celebrations of the inland towns and of their churches. In these discourses we find both of the opposing views presented. There are probably elements of truth in both, but as far as the general features of social life are concerned and their effect in stimulating or in depressing the individual, the latter view seems to be more in accord with the facts as we know them.

The Rev. Mr. Storrs, in reviewing a pastorate of fifty years in the town of Braintree, Mass., said: "And when it is remembered that fifty years ago, and for many after years, no post office blessed the town, nor public conveyance for letters, papers, or persons, was to be had, even semi-weekly, except through villages two miles distant; that but for the occasional rumbling of a butcher's cart, or a trades-man's wagon, the fall of the hammer on the lap-stone, or the call of the plowman to his refractory team, our streets had well nigh rivaled the graveyard in silence, it can scarcely surprise one, that our knowledge of the outer world was imperfect, nor that general intelligence and enterprise was held at a discount; and if powder, kettle drums, and conch-shells, proclaimed the celebration of a wedding; or if wine, and 'spirits more dangerous than any from the vasty deep,' were imbibed at funerals to quiet the nerves and move the lachrymals of attendants; or if rowdyism and fisticuffs triumphed over law and order on town meeting, muster and election days, ... it was but the legitimate outflow of combined ignorance and heaven daring recklessness. Those days are passed and shame throws its thick mantle over them."[1]

Tendencies Toward Social Degeneration.

An isolated community always tends toward social degeneration, and the drunkenness, rowdyism, and general coarseness of manners of the inland towns at this time were but premonitions of the more disastrous results which might be expected from economic and social stagnation. At no time in these communities was there a distinct criminal class, of the type now technically known as degenerate; but petty crimes, stealing, assaults and disturbances were of frequent occurrence.[2] There are many indications that the influence of the church was decadent. Up to the beginning of the nineteenth century, the ecclesiastical organization had secured, by means of a censorship of the private life of its members so inquisitorial as to seem nowadays intolerable, fairly submissive adherence to a rigid code of morality. With the decline in the authority of the church in matters of doctrine came also a weakening in its control over the conduct of its adherents.[3]

Another cause of laxity in morals, of probably greater importance, was the general spirit of lawlessness spreading over the country after the Revolution, which seems especially to have affected the country districts. The soldiers returning from the war found it hard to settle down and get their living honestly in the previous humdrum routine. They brought back with them new and often vicious habits which the rest of the community imitated. Then, in the interval between the overturn of the regularly constituted colonial authori-

---

[1] Fiftieth Anniversary of the Ordination and Settlement of Richard S. Storrs, D.D., Pastor of the First Congregational Church in Braintree, Mass. July 3, 1861. Boston, 1861. pp. 32–33.

[2] The records of the town courts, where accessible, are a rich source of evidence on this point. See Wood, Sumner Gilbert. The Taverns and Turnpikes of Old Blanford, pp. 188–205.

[3] Dwight, Travels, IV. 380, writes: "Crimes, to a considerable extent are now practised, avowed, and vindicated, are made the materials of a jest, and gloried in as proofs of ingenuity and independence, which our ancestors knew only by report, and of which they spoke only with horror. Inferior deviations from rectitude are become extensively familiar, and regarded as things of course." The cause which the writer ascribes for this state of things is the growing spirit of infidelity. He adds: "From these and other causes, we have lost that prompt energy in behalf of what is right, and that vigorous hostility to what is wrong, which were so honourable traits in the character of those who have gone before us." (p. 381).

ties and the establishment of the national government under the new federal constitution, there was a period of semi-anarchy, when obedience to any sort of law was difficult to enforce. The disrespect for authority in both church and state which arose from these conditions could not fail to have a distinctly bad influence on the moral conditions in inland towns. In the disturbances of those days the inland farmer was generally to be found on the side of rebellion, and active in opposing a reëstablishment of law and order.[1]

Virtues of the Age of Homespun.

Too much emphasis must not be laid upon the dark features of the community life of these times. Undoubtedly there were many advantages arising from the homogeneous construction of society, from the uniformity of the inhabitants in race, religion and manners, and from the absence of class distinctions based on differences in wealth. The inland villages were by no means entirely lacking in opportunities for helpful and stimulating social intercourse; but it was from the home rather than from the community life that the principal virtues of the agricultural population, of which their descendants have been so justly proud, were chiefly derived. First of all, no child could grow up in the self-sufficient household of those days without being thoroughly trained in habits of frugality and economy. In his sermon, "The Age of Homespun," Horace Bushnell wrote: "It was also a great point, in this homespun mode of life that it imparted exactly what many speak of only with contempt, a closely girded habit of economy. Harnessed, all together, in the producing process, young and old, male and female, from the boy that rode the plow-horse, to the grandmother knitting under her spectacles, they had no conception of squandering lightly what they had all been at work, thread by thread, and grain by grain, to produce. They knew too exactly what every thing cost, even small things, not to husband them carefully."[2]

This frugality did at times develop into meanness, but not necessarily so; and whatever tendencies may have existed in this direction were to a certain degree offset by another characteristic which such households and such communities developed, that of mutual helpfulness. In a community where the services of the specialized pro-

---

[1] Take, for instance, Shay's Rebellion in Massachusetts, 1786–1787. See Fiske, John. *The Critical Period in American History.* Boston. 1898, pp. 192–198.

[2] *Work and Play,* p. 395.

fessions to which we are accustomed, such as those of the trained nurse or of the funeral director, for instance, were entirely lacking, the deficiency was made up by the voluntary offices of neighbors. It was turn and turn about. Such services were rarely if ever paid for, but the understanding was that the person or family receiving the service stood ready to render similar services willingly when occasion should arise. The practices of neighborly coöperation in the extraordinary tasks of farm labor, such as in raising buildings and in "changing works" of all sorts; the custom of parceling out portions of slaughtered animals so as to equalize consumption and decrease waste; all these arrangements were, we have seen, direct results of the farmers' necessity of adapting themselves to the self-sufficient conditions of their life. Indirectly, a helpful and neighborly spirit was stimulated.

Educative Effects.

In its educative effects the self-sufficient household produced certain results which the more formal training of our modern homes and schools has never been able to approximate. In the first place, it inculcated habits of self-reliance and an ability to bear responsibility. In large families where the various tasks of the house and farm were apportioned to each member of the family according to his strength and ability, even the little children were taught early that for the performance of their particular tasks they were to be strictly accountable. It was a hard discipline often, and perhaps it developed too early a serious way of taking life, but under proper control it evolved a race of men strong and independent.

The Importance of the Mechanical Ingenuity of the Yankee Farmer in the Future Industrial Development of New England.

We have already spoken of the mechanical ingenuity of the Yankee farmer. It arose just as immediately as these other characteristics from the necessities of getting a complete living from the products of a single farm, and from the lack of any clearly marked division of labor in the rural communities.[1] Of the many contributions of the

---

.[1] It may be objected that there have been many cases of isolated communities whose inhabitants have not shown themselves especially ingenious along mechanical lines. Instances coming readily to mind are the Boers of the Transvaal and the mountaineers of eastern Tennessee. But it will be found that such communities were in many important respects not comparable with the towns of southern New England. Although suffering under the same inability to export foodstuffs, and consequently feeling the same necessity of making use of ingen-

Age of Homespun to the future industrial development of New England, this characteristic of mechanical ingenuity was perhaps the most important. The stage of self-sufficiency was in many ways a period of preparation for the coming era. The land had all been cleared and settled; a considerable amount of capital had been accumulated in the commercial towns, ready for investment in new enterprises which might prove more successful than commerce; stable and efficient legal and political institutions had been organized; and finally the population had been trained in habits of frugality, economy and industry. But it was the presence of inventive ingenuity which seems to have aided the growth of manufacturing in New England more than any of these. The ability to devise a means to an end; to invent and perfect all sorts of tools and appliances, was originally turned to account only in more efficiently supplying the needs of the household or the surrounding community. When, however, the growing prosperity of the cotton planters in the Southern states opened a market for manufactured goods; when the ingenious farmer-mechanics of the inland towns of southern New England learned that they could get a living, and a much better living than that derived from agriculture by the sale of the fruits of their skill over a wide area, then this inventive ingenuity became utilized in the establishment and development of numberless enterprises and showed itself as a most valuable asset in industrial progress.

ious contrivances in satisfying their own wants, these three communities differed widely in the advantages of education, of communal life and perhaps also in the inborn qualities of their people. Neither the colonists of the South African republic, nor the rural folk of the Tennessee mountains enjoyed the widespread common-school education with its consequent high level of intelligence, nor the close association in village communities, both of which must have favored the development of intellectual talents of all sorts,—among them inventiveness,—among the Yankee farmers. It may be also that the original settlers of New England, coming as they did largely from urban districts in the mother country, transmitted to their descendants a superior knowledge of the technical processes of the ordinary crafts, and perhaps certain favoring physiological and psychological characteristics.

More important than these considerations, in my opinion, is the fact that the commercial isolation of the New England towns was not as complete as that of the other two communities mentioned. For their foodstuffs, the farmers of the inland towns of southern New England had practically no market. For small manufactured wares, however, there was a market in the coast towns and in the Southern states. Consequently in the production of wooden-ware and tin-ware, of hats and shoes, of buttons, clocks and other Yankee notions for these markets, opportunity was given for the full fruition of that mechanical ingenuity which germinated in the favoring atmosphere of the self-sufficient farms.

The Home Market.

With the growth of manufactures in the inland towns of southern New England came the rise of a specialized non-agricultural population and a market for the farmer was created, not far away in the Southern states or in the West Indies, but right at home, often in his own town. And thus came to an end the Age of Homespun, the era of commercial isolation. It was not a change accomplished in a single decade; in many out-of-the-way villages conditions remained practically constant until 1840 or 1850; but in 1810 an era of change had set in. From that time to the Civil War an Industrial Revolution was in progress, comparable in scope and in its effects to that which had preceded it by a half-century in England.

APPENDIX A.

Population Statistics of Southern New England. 1810.

Table I.

Population by States.

Massachusetts	*472,040
Connecticut	261,942
Rhode Island	76,931
Total	810,913

* Not including Maine.

Table II.

Population in Towns Grouped According to Size.

	NO. TOWNS IN GROUP	POPULATION OF GROUP	PER CENT OF TOTAL POPULATION
Group A. Towns over 10,000	3	56,000	6.90
Group B. Towns 5,000–10,000	11	68,500	8.45
Group C. Towns 3,000– 5,000	38	141,800	17.50
Group D. Towns under 3,000	385	544,700	67.15
Total, all groups	437	811,000	100.00

Table III.

Population of the Towns in the Various Groups.

Group A.

Boston, Mass.	33,250
Salem, Mass.	12,673
Providence, R. I.	10,071

Group B.

New Bedford, Mass.	5,651
Gloucester, Mass.	5,943
Marblehead, Mass.	5,900
Newbury, Mass.	5,176
Newburyport, Mass.	7,634
Nantucket, Mass.	6,807
Bridgewater, Mass.	5,157
Hartford, Conn.	6,003
Middletown, Conn.	5,382
New Haven, Conn.	6,967
Newport, R. I.	7,907

TABLE III—*Continued.*

Group C.

Barnstable, Mass.	3,446
Dartmouth, Mass.	3,219
Rehoboth, Mass.	4,866
Taunton, Mass.	3,907
Andover, Mass.	3,164
Beverly, Mass.	4,608
Danvers, Mass.	3,127
Ipswich, Mass.	3,569
Lynn, Mass.	4,087
West Springfield, Mass.	3,109
Charlestown, Mass.	4,959
Roxbury, Mass.	3,669
Middleborough, Mass.	4,400
Plymouth, Mass.	4,228
Scituate, Mass.	3,000
Brookfield, Mass.	3,170
Chatham, Conn.	3,258
Danbury, Conn.	3,606
East Hartford, Conn.	3,240
East Windsor, Conn.	3,081
Fairfield, Conn.	4,125
Greenwich, Conn.	3,553
Groton, Conn.	4,451
Guilford, Conn.	3,845
Litchfield, Conn.	4,639
Lyme, Conn.	4,321
New London, Conn.	3,238
New Milford, Conn.	3,537
Norwalk, Conn.	3,000
Norwich, Conn.	3,528
Preston, Conn.	3,284
Saybrook, Conn.	3,996
Stamford, Conn.	4,440
Stonington, Conn.	3,043
Wethersfield, Conn.	3,961
Warwick, R. I.	3,757
Smithfield, R. I.	3,828
South Kingston, R. I.	3,560

APPENDIX B.

Emigration from the Inland Towns in Southern New England. 1720–1820.

Shifting of Population Within Southern New England—1720–1775.

There had been a steady expansion of population in Massachusetts from the oldest settlements on the coast toward new lands to the westward, until by 1720 all the best land east of the Connecticut Valley had been occupied. The new home-seekers wanted not only land but good land; hence many parts of Worcester County were left unsettled until a later period.[1] In Connecticut the oldest settlements along the Connecticut River at Hartford, Windsor and Wethersfield, and the colony at New Haven, had radiated their surplus in all directions. Before 1720, however, most of the emigrants from these original settlements had gone to the east and the north where they met the settlers from Massachusetts and filled up the townships in Windham, Tolland and New London Counties. About 1720 or 1730 the pressure of population began to be felt in this region, too, and the tide of emigration swung to the west and northwest. Litchfield County in Connecticut then became the destination of the surplus. So we find in the years 1719–1721 families from Lebanon joining with those from Hartford and Windsor in settling the new town of Litchfield.[2] A similar instance of the joining of the streams of emigration from the newer eastern towns with those from the first settlements is found in the settlement of Sharon by families from Colchester and Lebanon together with families from New Haven.[3]

The Connecticut emigrants did not, however, remain in Litchfield County until all its lands had been taken up, but following along up the Housatonic Valley, they invaded the new lands in Berkshire and Hampshire Counties in western Massachusetts, meeting there the families arriving from eastern Massachusetts, as well as some Dutch emigrants from New York. Se we find in the town of Wales settlers from Salem, Palmer and Grafton in Massachusetts and from Windham, Tolland and Union in Connecticut. In New Marlborough emigrants from Northampton and Dedham in Massachusetts met with those from Canterbury and Suffield in Connecticut; in Sandisfield the colonists were from Enfield and Wethersfield and from Cape Cod towns.[4] In this early colonization Rhode Island seems

---

[1] See Mathews, Lois Kimball. The Expansion of New England. Boston, 1909. p. 79.

[2] Ibid. p. 92.

[3] Pease and Niles, Gazetteer, p. 261. This settlement was made in 1738–1739. From Durham, in Hartford County, settlers went to Torrington in 1737. See Fowler, W. C., History of Durham. Hartford, 1867, p. 209. This town lost so steadily by emigration that its population increased from 1,076 in 1774 to only 1,101 in 1810.

[4] Mathews, Op. cit., pp. 79–80.

to have taken little part. It had but a little over 7,000 people in 1708, and although much of its soil was unfertile, yet its commercial interests were so prosperous in this period that it succeeded in retaining nearly all of its natural increase. Consequently its population increased very rapidly, amounting to over 40,000 in 1755.[1]

Beginning of Movement to Northern New England.

In 1760 emigration began in earnest to lands outside the borders of the states of southern New England. The fall of Quebec in 1758 brought the war between England and France in this country practically to an end. With the fear of hostile attack, especially from the Indians, thus removed, large numbers of settlers began to move into the northern states. In New Hampshire, between 1760 and 1775, one hundred new towns were planted by colonists from Massachusetts, Rhode Island and Connecticut. In Maine, ninety-four towns were founded between 1759 and 1776, principally by settlers from Massachusetts. In Vermont in the same period seventy-four new towns were settled.[2] Connecticut people went in great numbers to new homes along the upper valley of their great river, often giving the new town the name of the old home from which they had come. In Vermont alone there are now forty towns whose names repeat those of Connecticut.[3]

Even before the Revolution, the Delaware and Susquehanna companies had been organized in Connecticut and had conveyed hundreds of families from that state to new lands in northeastern Pennsylvania. The craze for emigration had led to an ill-fated attempt of some four hundred families from towns on the Connecticut River to colonize lands on the Yazoo River in Mississippi. A temporary check to the outward movement is observable during the Revolution. Even before the conclusion of peace, however, a veritable rush of emigration began to new lands in the West, in New York state and in Ohio.[4] In Pease and Niles' description of Connecticut we read: "The spirit of emigration which has prevailed so extensively in this State, disclosed itself previously to the Revolutionary war; emigration at this period being directed to the present counties of Dutchess and Columbia, in the State of New York, and the counties bordering upon Connecticut River in the State of New Hampshire. After the war, the spirit of emigration revived, and was principally directed to the western section of New Hampshire, and the territory now comprising the State of Vermont; a large proportion of the original inhabitants of these sections of our country being from Connecticut. Within the last thirty years (written in 1819),

---

[1] Censuses were taken in Rhode Island in 1708, 1730, 1748, 1755, 1774, 1776, 1782. These were all reprinted in the Report on the Census of Rhode Island, 1865. Prepared by Edwin M. Snow, Providence, 1867, p. xxxii.

[2] These facts are from Mathews, Expansion of New England, pp. 108–115.

[3] See Memorial History of Hartford County, I. 203.

[4] The inland newspapers such as the Massachusetts Spy, the Windham Herald, the Pittsfield Sun, and the Litchfield Monitor contain regularly advertisements of lands for sale in New York, Pennsylvania, Virginia, and Ohio in the years 1800–1810. The advertisements of farms for sale in the New England towns in which these papers were printed, show the process of exchange of old for new land which was taking place.

the current of emigration from this State has swelled to a torrent, and has been directed principally to the westward."[1] This movement continued in great volume until checked, temporarily, by the growth of manufactures in the decades after 1810.

Volume of Emigration Shown by Early Census Figures.

The results of this wholesale movement of people are observable in a comparison of early census figures in the states of southern New England. In Connecticut the earliest census was taken in 1756.[2] It gave the total population of the colony as 129,925 persons. At the next census, 1774,[3] this number had increased to 197,872, showing a growth of 52 per cent in eighteen years, a decennial rate of increase of 29 per cent. If we assume that population was in reality increasing at this period at a rate very near the physiological maximum, that is, doubling itself every twenty-five years, we may take the "natural" rate of increase to have been about 40 per cent in each decade. This would lead us to believe that even at that early date the state was losing about 11 per cent of its decennial increase.

The same state of affairs prevailed in Rhode Island. From 1708 to 1755 the increase was very rapid, as we have seen, averaging about 107 per cent per decennium. In the years 1755 to 1774 the population increased from 40,414 to 59,707, or at a decennial rate of 25.1 per cent.[4] Emigration was evidently taking place from this state in even greater volume than from Connecticut.

Massachusetts was increasing in this period more rapidly in population than either of her neighbors. Although she did not retain a larger proportion of her own annual increase, yet her loss from emigration was very nearly offset by her gains from the states on her southern borders. In 1764 the population of this state was 201,984;[5] and in 1784 it was 346,653.[6] The increase in these two decades was 71.6 per cent, or 35.8 per cent in each ten years.

After the Revolution.

A striking contrast is presented by an examination of the growth of population in these states after the Revolution. As we have seen, it was then that the emigrants from the older towns tended to push on beyond the boundaries of their own states and to settle in Northern or Western states. We are not surprised, therefore, to find that the population of Connecticut increased but 20.2 per cent in these sixteen years, at a decennial rate of 12.6 per cent, and that Rhode Island gained but 15.3 per cent in the same period, 9.6 per cent per decennium. In Massachusetts emigration was about as great in proportion to its population, for in the six years, 1784 to 1790, it increased but 9.3 per cent, or at a decennial

---

[1] Gazetteer, p. 11.

[2] Contained in Conn. Col. Public Records, Vol. XIV, p. 492.

[3] Ibid. pp. 485–491.

[4] These figures are from Snow, Census of Rhode Island, pp. xxxii.

[5] This census is reprinted in A Century of Population Growth, pp. 158–162.

[6] This figure is estimated by Dr. Chickering from the number of rateable and non-rateable polls returned by an enumeration in that year. See Chickering, Jesse. A Statistical View of the Population of Massachusetts from 1765 to 1840. Boston. 1846, p. 10.

rate of 11.6 per cent. Taking the combined figures for Rhode Island and Connecticut, we find that before the Revolution the population of these states was increasing at the rate of 28.4 per cent in each decade; after 1774 until 1790 the increase was only 11.9 per cent per decennium. This slackening in growth seems to have been due principally if not entirely to the increased emigration. The statistics for Massachusetts agree in general with these figures.

The continuance of emigration in the years 1790–1820 may be observed in the slow rate of growth of southern New England as compared with the increase of population throughout the United States.

TABLE I.[1]

	1790	1800	1810	1820
Massachusetts..........	378,787	422,845	472,040	523,287
Connecticut............	237,946	251,002	261,942	275,248
Rhode Island..........	68,825	69,122	76,931	83,059
Total................	685,558	742,969	810,913	881,594

The increase per cent in each decade was as follows:

TABLE II.

	1790 TO 1800	1800 TO 1810	1810 TO 1820
	per cent	*per cent*	*per cent*
Massachusetts......................	11.6	11.6	10.9
Connecticut.......................	5.5	4.4	5.1
Rhode Island......................	0.0	11.3	8.0
Southern New England..............	12.8	·9.1	8.7
United States......................	35.1	36.4	33.1

Statistical Estimate of Emigration, 1790–1820.

So great had this colonizing movement become by 1810 that a number of attempts had been made to estimate statistically its amount.[2] The method usually adopted was the application to these states of the rate of increase observed over the United States as a whole. Thus a figure was obtained which represented the population which these states would have had, had there been no emigration. The total increase in population throughout the country in the years 1790–1820 was 145.6 per cent. There seems no reason for believing that the natural increase was any less in southern New England than elsewhere. Certainly with such an outlet for surplus population as emigration afforded, and with such a readiness to emigrate as the inhabitants of these states displayed, there could have been but slight operation of any preventive check. Nor does it appear that the death

[1] These figures are from the Abstract of the 13th U. S. Census, pp. 24–25. As in all other computations in this essay, the figures for Massachusetts do not include the population of the District of Maine.

[2] As in Burdick, William. The Massachusetts Manual. Boston. 1814. I. 179; and in Blodget, Economica, p. 79.

rate was any higher here. In fact, the conditions were far more favorable for the survival of children than on the frontier. If we may assume that the population of Massachusetts, Rhode Island and Connecticut did increase by 145.6 per cent in the years 1790–1820, then, had there been no emigration, the census of 1820 would have shown a total for the three states of 1,681,673 persons. As a matter of fact this total was only 881,594. Consequently according to this computation the loss by emigration in the thirty years must have been 800,000 persons.

Economic Aspects of Emigration—Agricultural Regions Lost Most Heavily.

For the purposes of this essay our interest in this movement of population is centered in its relations to the economic conditions prevailing in the country towns. Is there any evidence to show that the purely agricultural inland regions were affected more or less than those on the rivers and on the coast? If so, what light do these differences shed on the causes of emigration?

There is an abundance of evidence to prove that the counties and towns on the rivers and the coast lost far less by emigration than the inland country. Taking three inland counties in Connecticut, Litchfield, Windham and Tolland; we find that their total population amounted in 1790 to 80,782. Twenty years later,[1] it was 81,285, an increase of 503 persons or $\frac{6}{10}$ of one per cent. In the same period two coast counties and one river county, Fairfield, New Haven and Hartford, increased from 105,109 to 122,747, or 16.8 per cent.

TABLE III.

Population Growth in Inland and Coast Counties.

	INLAND COUNTIES		
	1790	1800	1810
Litchfield..........................	38,755	41,214	41,375
Windham..........................	28,921	28,222	26,111
Tolland...........................	13,106	14,319	13,799
Total..........................	80,782	83,755	81,285

	COAST AND RIVER COUNTIES		
Fairfield...........................	36,250	38,208	40,950
Hartford..........................	38,029	42,147	44,733
New Haven........................	30,830	32,162	37,064
Total..........................	105,109	112,517	122,747

[1] I have limited the inquiry to the two decades because of the influence which the growth of manufactures was already beginning to exert in the decade 1810–1820. In the case of Tolland and Windham counties there were some changes in boundary lines between 1790 and 1810; the figures given are for the areas as of 1790.

Narrowing the scope of our inquiry to the towns, we find the same situation. Wherever there was a chance for some additional employment for the inhabitants besides agriculture, there the loss from emigration was much less than in purely agricultural towns. Contrast, for instance, the towns of Farmington and Danbury in Connecticut. The former, situated in a rich river valley,[1] contained in 1790 2,700 people, who got their living entirely from agriculture. In 1810, twenty years later, the population was 2,750; the increase had been less than 2 per cent. In Danbury there was in 1790 a population of 3,031. In 1810 there were 3,606 persons on the same area. The increase in twenty years was almost 20 per cent. As far as the productivity of the agricultural industry was concerned, both towns were on an equal footing.[2] In area Farmington had clearly the advantage, containing 70 square miles while Danbury had only 58.[3] The reason why a large part of the surplus of population stayed at home in Danbury while almost all the growing generation emigrated from Farmington is to be found in the presence in the former of a manufacturing enterprise, the hatters' shops.[4]

Population Changes in Commercial and Inland Towns.

The same sort of contrast is found between commercial and inland towns. Such towns as New Haven, Providence, Salem and Boston gained rapidly in population and do not seem to have been in any appreciable degree affected by the emigration which was draining the backcountry districts.[5] Here we find the growing prosperity of commerce as a force retaining the natural increase of population. But even the small towns along the coast, where, as we have seen, there was not enough commercial business to employ any considerable proportion of the population, grew steadily during this period. Consider, for example, the contrast between the towns of Lebanon and Greenwich, in Connecticut. Both of these towns included about the same area, 50 square miles. The inhabitants of both were mainly farmers; those in Lebanon entirely so, and in Greenwich with the exception of the owners of twelve or fifteen small sloops trading to New York. In the years 1790–1810 the population of Lebanon decreased from 4,156 to 3,414, a loss of over 20 per cent; in the same years Greenwich had increased from 3,175 to 3,553, a gain of nearly 12 per cent. The decline of the former town cannot be explained on the ground that its soil was less fertile than that of the latter.[6] The explanation of this difference is to be found in the fact that the farmers of

---

[1] For a description of Farmington see Pease and Niles, Gazetteer, p. 71.

[2] Pease and Niles, Gazetteer, pp. 176–178.

[3] Op. cit., loc. cit.

[4] See supra pp. 269-270. Another inland town which increased steadily in this period was Berlin, the center of the tinware manufacture. Its population in 1790 was 2,465; in 1810 it was 2,900.

[5] The increase in population of New Haven 1790–1810 amounted to 55 per cent; in Providence the gain was 57 per cent. Boston gained 86 per cent and Salem 59 per cent.

[6] Of agricultural conditions in Lebanon we read: "The soil is generally a rich deep, unctuous mould, nearly of a chocolate colour; it is very fertile and peculiarly adapted to grass." Pease and Niles, art. Lebanon.

Greenwich had a market close at hand in the city of New York,[1] easily accessible by water transportation on the Sound; whereas Lebanon was fifteen or more miles from Norwich, the nearest port.

The Influence of a Market for Foodstuffs.

In Massachusetts a similar contrast may be made between the towns of Brookfield in Worcester County, and Waltham in Middlesex County.[2] In the matter of area and in fertility of soil Brookfield seems to have had the advantage. Neither town had any industrial or manufacturing enterprises, beyond the usual artisans' shops found in every inland town.[3] The population changes in these towns in the years 1790–1810 were, in spite of these similarities, quite different. In Brookfield a population of 3,100 persons increased to 3,170; in Waltham there were at the first date 882 people and at the second 1,014. The gain in one case was between 2 and 3 per cent and in the other almost 15 per cent. The explanation is found again in the presence of a market accessible to the farmers of Waltham. This market they found in Boston, only ten miles distant, whereas their colleagues in Brookfield were fifty-five miles farther away. That this market was in fact influential in increasing the prosperity and the productiveness of the agricultural industry in Waltham is apparent from the description of a contemporary writer. He says: "As most of the inhabitants are farmers, and cultivate their farms with a view to the constant supply of the market of the metropolis, the fruits of their labours are various . . . . The state of agriculture has been improving among our farmers, for several years. The residence of gentleman farmers in this town and vicinity has undoubtedly contributed to this improvement; but the chief causes are the increasing demands of the market and the enhancing price of labour, which have taught the owners of the soil, that it is more profitable to cultivate a few acres highly, than many in the ordinary way."[4]

Summary of Population Changes, 1790–1820.

In summarizing the movement of population in the three southern states of New England in the period 1720–1820 we find: (1) In the forty years, 1720–1760, emigration was confined largely within the borders of the states, resulting merely in a redistribution, a shifting of the surplus from the older towns to new lands in the western counties. (2) After 1760 this process of settling new land within these states continued with great rapidity, but some of the more adventurous colonists were already moving out to found new towns in northern New England and in states to the westward. (3) Where as, up to the Revolution, this emigration to more distant regions had assumed no very great proportions, after peace had been concluded it began with new vigor and from that time until

---

[1] Pease and Niles say of the coasting trade of this town: "This trade is a great convenience to the farmers, as it affords them a great facility for conveying their produce to New York. Gazetteer, p. 180.

[2] The facts regarding Waltham are from the description of that town contained in Mass. Hist. Soc. Coll., II. 3: 261–284; for Brookfield from Whitney's History of the County of Worcester, pp. 62–82.

[3] The cotton mills were first established in Waltham in 1812 and 1813. Mass. Hist. Soc. Coll., loc. cit.

[4] Mass. Hist. Soc. Coll., II. 3: 262–263.

1820 continued at such a rate as to leave the population of these states practically stationary. (4) The migratory movement was felt much more strongly in inland counties than on the coast, because of the entire reliance of the former on agriculture. (5) Among the agricultural towns, those which had a market for their products suffered far less severely from emigration than other towns not so favorably situated.

Emigration the Result of a Crippled State of Agriculture.

In this phenomenon of emigration, therefore, we have another feature of the social and economic life of southern New England which was caused directly by the dependence of the entire community on a single industry, agriculture. There was, as we have seen, no division of labor sufficient either to furnish a market for agricultural products within the rural town, or to create a non-agricultural population in industrial towns and cities. There was, indeed, a small market in the commercial towns on the coast and another somewhat larger in the West Indies and the Southern states, but their combined demands were not sufficient to influence to any appreciable degree the life of the farmers in inland towns. The results of this state of affairs upon the agricultural industry are considered in Chapter V. List has called this condition "a crippled state of agriculture," and goes on to show how the inevitable result is emigration. He says: "By a *crippled state of agriculture*[1] we mean that state of things in which, from want of a powerful and steadily developing manufacturing industry, the entire increase of population tends to throw itself on agriculture for employment, consumes all the surplus agricultural production of the country, and as soon as it has considerably increased either has to emigrate or share with the agriculturists already in existence the land immediately at hand, till the landed property of every family has become so small that it produces only the most elementary and necessary portion of that family's requirements of food and raw materials, but no considerable surplus which it might exchange with the manufacturers for the manufactured products which it requires."[2]

That the causes of this great loss of population were essentially economic was realized by contemporary writers. Various travelers had remarked that the southern states in New England were, at the end of the eighteenth century, fully settled. For instance, La Rochefoucauld wrote: "Connecticut, Rhode Island and Massachusetts have at present nearly their due quantum of population."[3] One especially clear-minded writer had, as early as 1789, anticipated the only remedy for the outward movement. He wrote: "Our lands are cleared and settled; our farms in general will not bear a further division; unless there be some new resource, our most active, industrious and enterprising young men . . . . will emigrate to those new parts of the continent where there is more vacant territory."[4]

---

[1] Author's italics.

[2] List, Friedrich. The National System of Political Economy. Translated by S. S. Lloyd. London. 1885. pp. 154–155.

[3] Travels, II. 195. See also Carey, American Pocket Atlas, p. 46; Morse, Gazetteer, 1810, art. Connecticut; American Husbandry, I. 47.

[4] Quoted from an anonymous letter dated at Hartford, Connecticut, printed in the American Museum. Vol. VIII., p. 25.

Other Causes of Emigration.

Combined with the economic motive, the demand for new soil, were undoubtedly others more psychological in nature. Some men were unable to fit into the rigid, Puritanical social and ecclesiastical systems. They emigrated in order to breathe the freer, more unconventional atmosphere of the pioneer communities. Others were simply infected by the contagious spirit; their friends had gone or were going; they too wanted to see the new country and to live its new life. Dwight takes account of these and other motives in the following passage from his Travels: "In the formation of colonies, those, who are first inclined to emigrate, are usually such as have met with difficulties at home. These are commonly joined by persons, who, having large families and small farms, are induced, for the sake of settling their children comfortably, to seek for new and cheaper lands. To both are always added the discontented, the enterprising, the ambitious, and the covetous. Many of the first, and some of all these classes, are found in every new American country, within ten years after its settlement has commenced. From this period, kindred, friendship, and former neighbourhood, prompt others to follow them. Others, still, are allured by the prospect of gain, presented in every new country to the sagacious, from the purchase and sale of new lands; while not a small number are influenced by the brilliant stories, which everywhere are told concerning most tracts during the early progress of their settlement."[1]

---

[1] Travels, II. 439. In the succeeding pages, 439–443, one may read a description of the successive stages in the settlement of new land, from pioneering to ultimate cultivation in well-settled communities, which has attained the rank of a classic in economic history.

APPENDIX C.

A. General Works.

BORDLEY, JOHN BEALE. Essays on Husbandry and Rural Affairs. Philadelphia. 1791. 536 pp. 2 ed. 1801.

BOWLER, METCALF. Treatise on Agriculture and Practical Husbandry. Providence. 1786.

DABNEY, J. Address to Farmers. pp. 64. Salem. 1796.

DEANE, SAMUEL. The New England Farmer; or, Georgical Dictionary: pp. 335. Worcester. 1790. 2 ed. 1797 (3 ed. 1822).

ELIOT, JARED. Essays on Field Husbandry in New England. Boston. 1760. 2 ed. 1761.

ENFIELD, EDWARD. An Inquiry in to the State of Farms: to the Farmers of New Hampshire. Boston. 1812.

EVERETT, DAVID. Common Sense in Dishabille: or, The Farmer's Monitor. Worcester. 1799.

GLEANINGS from the Most Celebrated Book on Husbandry. Philadelphia. 1803.

HIRZEL, HANS KASPAR. The Rural Socrates. Hallowell (Me.). 1800.

HUNTER, A. Georgical Essays. 6 vols. New York. 1803–1804.

MOORE, T. Gross Error of American Agriculture Exposed. Baltimore. 1801.

PARKINSON, RICHARD. The Experienced Farmer. Philadelphia. 1799.

ROBERTS, JOB. The Pennsylvania Farmer. Philadelphia. 1804.

SPURRIERS, —— The Practical Farmer. Worcester. 1792.

TAYLOR, COL. JOHN. Arator. Baltimore. 3 ed. 1817.

(THOMPSON, CHARLES) Notes on Farming, pp. 38. New York. 1787.

WARREN, GENERAL J(ames) Observations on Agriculture. In American Museum. Vol. II. 1788.

B. Special Works.

ABSTRACT of a Late Treatise on Hemp. Boston. 1766.

AFFERT, M. The Art of Preserving Animal and Vegetable Substances. New York. 1812.

ANDERSON, JAMES. Essay on Quick Lime as a Manure. Boston. 1799.

BORDLEY, JOHN BEALE. Comparative View of the Crops of England and Maryland. Philadelphia. 1784.

> Sketches of a Rotation of Crops. 1797.
>
> Treatise of Country Habitations. 1798.
>
> Essays and Notes on American Husbandry. 1799.
>
> Treatise on the Culture of Hemp. 1799.
>
> Queries on the Nature and Principles of Vegetation. 1800.

---

[1] This list has been taken largely from that given in U. S. Department of Agriculture, Annual Report, 1868, pp. 597–607.

CUSTIS, G. W. P.　Importance of Encouraging Agriculture.　Alexandria.　1808.

"FARMER OF MASSACHUSETTS."　Complete Guide for the Management of Bees.　Worcester.　1792.

GRIFFEN, WILLIAM.　Treatise on the Cultivation of the Pineapple.　Newark (N. J.).　1808.

—— ——　Hemp.　Observations on its Culture.　Boston.　1766.

LOGAN, GEORGE.　Experiments with the Best Rotation of Crops.　Philadelphia.　1807.

LIVINGSTON, ROBERT R.　Essay on Sheep.　New York.　1809.　2 ed.　1810.

MANN, THOMAS.　Culture of the Young Thorn.　Wilmington (Del.)　1807.

MINOR, (THADDEUS).　The Experienced Bee Keeper.　Litchfield (Conn.)　1804.

RUSH, BENJAMIN.　An Account of the Sugar Maple Tree of the United States.　Philadelphia.　1792.

—— ——　Treatise on Silk Worms.　New York.　1793.

PETERS, RICHARD.　Agricultural Inquiries on Plaster of Paris.　Philadelphia.　1797.

REDD, GEORGE.　Treatise on Fertilizing Poor and Exhausted Lands.　Winchester (Va.).　1809.

TWANLEY, J.　Dairying Exemplified.　Providence.　1796.

BIBLIOGRAPHY.

ADAMS, CHARLES FRANCIS. Three Episodes in Massachusetts History. 2 vols. Boston. 1892.

ADAMS, HENRY. History of the United States. 1801–1817. 10 vols. New York. 1889–1891.

—— —— American Husbandry. 2 vols. London. 1775.

AMERICAN Museum; or Universal Magazine: 12 vols. Printed by M. Carey. Philadelphia. 1787–1792.

ANDREWS, CHARLES M. The River Towns of Connecticut. Baltimore. 1889. In Johns Hopkins University Studies in History and Political Science. 7th Series. VII.–IX.

APPLETON's Cyclopedia of American Biography. 7 vols. New York. 1887–1900.

APPLICATION for a Branch of the Bank of the United States in Hartford. (1817). MS. in library of Connecticut Historical Society, Hartford, Connecticut.

BACON, EDWIN M. The Connecticut River. New York. 1906.

BAILEY, JAMES M. History of Danbury, Connecticut. New York. 1896.

BAILEY, L. H. Cyclopedia of American Agriculture. 4 vols. New York. 1910.

BELKNAP, JEREMY. History of New Hampshire. 3 vols. Boston. 1791–1792.

BISHOP, J. LEANDER. History of American Manufactures. 2 vols. Philadelphia. 1861.

BLODGET, SAMUEL, JR. Economica: A Statistical Manual for the United States of America. Washington. 1806.

BOND, PHINEAS. Letters of . . . British Consul at Philadelphia. 1787–1794. In American Historical Association Annual Report. 1896–7.

BRISSOT DE WARVILLE, J. P. New Travels in the United States of America. English translation. London. 1792.

BROWN, ALEXANDER CAMPBELL. Colony Commerce. London. (ca. 1790.)

BÜCHER, KARL. Die Entstehung der Volkswirtschaft. 9te Auflage. Tübingen. 1910.

BURDICK, WILLIAM. The Massachusetts Manual. Boston. 1814.

BUSHNELL, REV. HORACE. Work and Play; or Literary Varieties. New York. 1864.

CAREY, MATTHEW. American Pocket Atlas. 3 edition. Philadelphia. 1805.

CHASTELLUX, FRANÇOIS JEAN, Marquis de. Travels in North America. 2 vols. London. 1788.

CHICKERING, JESSE. A Statistical View of the Population of Massachusetts from 1765 to 1840. Boston. 1846.

CONNECTICUT, Colony of. Public Records, 1636–1776. 15 vols. Hartford. 1850–1890.

CONNECTICUT, State of. Public Statute Laws. Vol. I. Hartford. 1808.

CONNECTICUT, State of. Resolves and Private Laws. 1789–1836. Hartford. 1837.

COXE, TENCH. Digest of Manufactures (1814). American State Papers. Finance, II. 666–812.

COXE, TENCH. A View of the United States of America. London. 1794.

CREVECOEUR, ST. JOHN DE. Letters of an American Farmer. London. 1783.

DAVIS, W. T. (editor.) The New England States, their Constitutional, Judicial . . . and Industrial History. 4 vols. Boston. 1897.

DEANE, SAMUEL, A. M. The New England Farmer: or Georgical Dictionary. Worcester. 1790. (2 edition 1797; 3 edition 1822.)

DE PEYSTER, FREDERICK. Biographical Sketch of Robert R. Livingston. New York. 1876.

DICKINSON, RODOLPHUS. A Geographical and Statistical View of Massachusetts. Greenfield (Mass.) 1813.

DRAYTON, JOHN. A View of South Carolina. Charleston. 1802.

DUNCAN, JOHN M. Travels through the United States and Canada. 2 vols. New York. 1823.

DWIGHT, TIMOTHY. Travels in New England and New York. 4 vols. London. 1823.

DWIGHT, TIMOTHY. A Statistical Account of the City of New Haven. [New Haven. 1811.]

EARLE, ALICE MORSE. Home Life in Colonial Days. New York. 1898.

EDWARDS, BRYAN. History. . . of the British Colonies in the West Indies. 3 edition. 3 vols. London. 1801.

FIELD, D. D. A Statistical Account of the County of Middlesex in Connecticut. Published by the Connecticut Academy of the Arts and Sciences. Middletown. 1819.

FIELD, EDWARD. The Colonial Tavern. Providence. 1897.

FELT, JOSEPH. History of Ipswich, Essex and Hamilton (Mass.). Cambridge. 1834.

FISKE, JOHN. The Critical Period in American History. Boston. 1898.

FLINT, CHARLES LOUIS. Progress in Agriculture. In Eighty Years' Progress of the United States. Hartford. 1867.

FOLGER, WALTER, JR. Topographical Description of Nantucket. Massachusetts Historical Society Collections. Series I. Vol. 3, pp. 153–155.

FOWLER, W. C. History of Durham (Conn.). Hartford. 1867.

FRANKLIN, BENJAMIN. Works. (Sparks edition.) 10 vols. Boston. 1837–1844.

GALLATIN, A(LBERT). Report of the Secretary of the Treasury on the Subject of Public Roads and Canals. Washington. 1808.

GALLATIN, ALBERT. Report on Manufactures. (1810.) American State Papers. Finance, II. 425–439.

GOODRICH, REV. SAMUEL. Statistical Account of Ridgefield in the County of Fairfield (Conn.). MS. in library of the Connecticut Historical Society. Written ca. 1800.

HAMILTON, ALEXANDER. Report on Manufactures. (1791.) American State Papers. Finance, I. 123–148.

HAMMOND, M. B. The Cotton Industry. Publications of the American Economic Association. New Series. No. 1. New York. 1897.

HARRIOTT, LIEUTENANT JOHN. Struggles through Life. 2 vols. London. 1807.

HARTFORD County, Connecticut, Memorial History. (J. H. Trumbull, editor.) 2 vols. Boston. 1886.

HAYWARD, JOHN. Gazetteer of Massachusetts. Revised edition. Boston. 1849.

HAZARD, BLANCHE E. Organization of the Boot and Shoe Industry in Massachusetts before 1875. Quarterly Journal of Economics. Vol. XXVII., pp. 236–262.

HAZARD, THOMAS. Account Book. Published at Washington County Agricultural Fair Grounds. Rhode Island. 1892.

HILDRETH, RICHARD. History of the United States of America. Revised edition. 6 vols. New York. 1877–1880.

HOLLAND, JOSEPH GILBERT. History of Western Massachusetts. 2 vols. Springfield. 1855.

JEFFERSON, THOMAS. Notes on Virginia. (1787.) Boston. 1832.

JORDAN, G. W. Claims of the British West India Colonists. London. 1804.

KENDALL, EDWARD AUGUSTUS. Travels through the Northern Parts of the United States in the years 1807 and 1808. 3 vols. New York. 1809.

KITTREDGE, GEORGE LYMAN. The Old Farmer and His Almanack. Boston. 1904.

LAMBERT, JOHN. Travels in Lower Canada and North America. 2 vols. London 1810.

LARNED, ELLEN DOUGLAS. History of Windham County, Conn. 2 vols. Worcester (Mass.). 1874–1880.

LA ROCHEFOUCAULD-LIANCOURT, Duc de. Travels through the United States of North America. 2 vols. London. 1799.

LATHROP, WILLIAM G. The Brass Industry in Connecticut. New Haven. 1909.

LEES, JOHN. Journal. New York. 1768. Reprinted 1911.

LIST, FREDERICK. The National System of Political Economy. Translated by S. S. Lloyd. London. 1885.

LIVINGSTON, ROBERT R. American Agriculture. In Edinburgh Encyclopedia. First American edition. 18 vols. Philadelphia. 1832. Vol. I., pp. 332–341.

MACLEAR, ANNE B. Early New England Towns. New York. 1908.

MACMASTER, JOHN BACH. History of the People of the United States. 6 vols. New York. 1885–1913.

MARQUIS, J. C. An Economic History of Agriculture in New England since 1840. MS. Thesis, Purdue University. 1909.

MASSACHUSETTS Agricultural Repository and Journal. 10 vols. Boston. 1793–1832. Vols. I. and II. are also entitled Papers of the Massachusetts Society for Promoting Agriculture.

MASSACHUSETTS BAY, Province of. Acts & Resolves. 1691–1780. 5 vols. Boston. 1869.

MASSACHUSETTS, Commonwealth of. Perpetual Laws. Worcester. 1788.

MASSACHUSETTS, Commonwealth of. Private and Special Statutes. 3 vols. Boston. 1805.

MASSACHUSETTS Historical Society Collections. Boston. 1795–1915.

MASSACHUSETTS Society for Promoting Agriculture, Papers. See Massachusetts Agricultural Repository and Journal.

MATHEWS, LOIS KIMBALL. The Expansion of New England. Boston. 1909.

MEDFORD, MACALL. Oil without Vinegar, ... or British, American, and West Indian Interests Considered. London. 1807.

MERRILL, ELIPHALET and PHINEHAS. Gazetteer of the State of New Hampshire. Exeter (N. H.). 1817.

MILLER, EDWARD AND WELLS, FREDERIC P. History of Ryegate, Vermont. St. Johnsbury (Vt.). 1913.

MITCHELL, JOHN. The Present State of Great Britain and North America. London. 1767.

MORRIS, JAMES A. Statistical Account of Several Towns in the County of Litchfield. Published by the Connecticut Academy of the Arts and Sciences. New Haven. 1811.

MORSE, JEDIDIAH. The American Gazetteer. 3 edition. Boston. 1810.

MORSE, JEDIDIAH. The American Universal Geography. 6 edition. Boston. 1812.

NANTUCKET, Notes on. Massachusetts Historical Society Collections. Series II. Volume 3, pp. 18–38.

NEILSEN, PETER. Recollections of a Six Years Residence in The United States of America. Glasgow. 1830.

NEW ENGLAND—What it is and What it is to be. (George French, editor.) Boston. 1911.

NEW HAMPSHIRE Historical Society Collections. 10 vols. Concord and Manchester (N. H.). 1824–1893.

NORTH, S. N. D. The New England Wool Manufacture. In The New England States. Vol. I. pp. 188–276.

PEASE AND NILES. Gazetteer of the States of Connecticut and Rhode Island. Hartford. 1819.

PHILIPS, ULRICH B. Plantation and Frontier. Vols. I. and II. in A Documentary History of American Industrial Society. (John R. Commons, editor.) 10 vols. Cleveland, Ohio. 1910–1911.

PITKIN, TIMOTHY. A Statistical View of the Commerce of the United States of America. Hartford. 1816.

PORTER, NOAH. Historical Discourse Delivered before the Citizens of Farmington (Conn.). Hartford. 1841.

RAMSAY, DAVID. History of South Carolina. 3 vols. Charleston. 1809.

RHODE ISLAND, State of. Index to Acts and Resolves. 1758–1850.

RHODE ISLAND, State of. Public Laws. Revision of 1798. Providence. 1798.

ROGERS, REV. MEDAD. Account Book—1784–1822. MS. in New Haven County Historical Society, New Haven, Connecticut.

SEYBERT, ADAM. Statistical Annals . . . . of the United States of America. Philadelphia. 1818.

SHAMEL, A. D. Tobacco. Article in Cyclopedia of American Agriculture. Vol. II., pp. 639–653.

SILLIMAN, BENJAMIN. Remarks on a Short Tour between Hartford and Quebec. New Haven. 1820.

SINCLAIR, SIR JOHN. Correspondence. 2 vols. London. 1831.

SMITH, ADAM. The Wealth of Nations. (Everyman's edition.) 2 vols. New York.

SNOW, EDWIN M. Report on the Census of Rhode Island. Providence. 1867.

STORRS, RICHARD S., D.D. Continuance in the Ministry. A Discourse Delivered in the First Congregational Church, Braintree, Mass., July 3, 1861. Boston. 1861.

STRICKLAND, WILLIAM. Observations on the Agriculture of the United States. London. 1801.

SWANK, J. M. The Manufacture of Iron in New England. In The New England States. Vol. I., pp. 359–441.

TAUSSIG, F. W. Inventors and Money-Makers. New York. 1915.

[THOMPSON, CHARLES]. Notes on Farming. New York. 1787.

TROWBRIDGE, THOMAS RUTHERFORD. Ancient Maritime Interests of New Haven. In The New England States. Vol. I., pp. 780–788.

TUCKER, GEORGE. Progress of the United States. New York. 1843.

TUDOR, WILLIAM. Letters on the Eastern States. 2 edition. Boston. 1821.

UNITED STATES Census Office. 2nd Census. 1800. [Washington. 1801.]

UNITED STATES Department of Agriculture. Special Report on the History and Present Condition of the Sheep Industry of the United States. Prepared under the direction of Dr. D. E. Salmon. Washington. 1892. 52nd Congress. 2nd Session. Miscellaneous Documents. No. 105.

UNITED STATES Department of Commerce and Labor, Bureau of the Census. A Century of Population Growth. Washington. 1909.

UNITED STATES Library of Congress. Check List of American Eighteenth Century Newspapers. Washington. 1912.

WALKER, J. B. The Farm of the First Minister. Reprinted from Report of the New Hampshire State Board of Agriculture. 1894. Concord, N. H. 1895.

WANSEY, HENRY F. A. S. Journal of an Excursion to the United States of America in the summer of 1794. Salisbury (England.) 1796.

WARDEN, D. B. Statistical, Political and Historical Account of the United States of America. 3 vols. Edinburgh. 1819.

WARREN, GENERAL J(AMES). Observations on Agriculture. In American Museum. Vol. II. (1788), pp. 344–348.

WEEDEN, WILLIAM B. Economic and Social History of New England, 1620–1789. 2 vols. Boston. 1890.

WELD, IASAC, JR. Travels through the States of North America . . . . during the Years 1795, 1796, and 1797. 4 edition. 2 vols. London. 1807.

WHITNEY, PETER. History of the County of Worcester. Worcester (Mass.). 1793.

WILLIAMS, SAMUEL. The Natural and Civil History of Vermont. 2 edition. 2 vols. Burlington (Vt.). 1809.

WINTERBOTHAM, W. Historical, Geographical, Commercial, ... View of the United States of America. 4 vols. New York. 1796.

WOOD, S. G. Taverns and Turnpikes of Blanford (Mass.). Published by the author. 1908.

WORCESTER, J. E. Universal Gazetteer. 2 edition. Boston. 1823.

WRIGHT, C. W. Wool Growing and the Tariff. Harvard University Economic Studies. Vol. V. Cambridge. 1910.

Newspapers.

The dates refer to the issues consulted.

The Farmers Journal. Brookfield, Mass. 1799–1802.

The Greenfield Gazette. Greenfield, Mass. 1792–1815.

The Hampshire Gazette. Northampton, Mass. 1796–1815.

The Massachusetts Spy; or Worcester Gazette. Worcester, Mass. 1794–1795, 1807–1820.

The National Aegis. Worcester, Mass. 1802–1805.

The Pittsfield Sun.   Pittsfield, Mass.   1800–1815.
The Political Focus.   Leominster, Mass.   1798–1799.
The Political Repository.   Brookfield, Mass.   1791–1798.
The Western Star.   Stockbridge, Mass.   1789–1803.
The Bee.   New London, Conn.   1797–1802.
The Connecticut Courant.   Hartford, Conn.   1809–1810.
The Farmers Journal.   Danbury, Conn.   1790–1793.
The Middletown Gazette.   Middletown, Conn.   1802–1803.
The Windham Herald.   Windham, Conn.   1806, 1808–9, 1811, 1813.
The Eagle or Dartmouth Centinel.   Hanover, N. H.   1793–1799.
The Farmers Weekly Museum.   Walpole, N. H.   1797–1798.
The New Hampshire Recorder.   Keene, N. H.   1787–1790.